F*CK UP

~TO~

FABULOUS

Lessons Learned on The Journey

To Empowerment

KIM STORY

Foreword

I have known the author, Kim Story, since before she was born. Her parents and I became good friends while her father and I were in law school together.

If you met Kim today, you would have no idea of the trials and tribulations she withstood throughout her entire life. Honestly, I didn't either. She is my goddaughter and her mother is one of my best friends, and yet, I didn't know. Maybe some of it, but not as much as I would have thought. Maybe there is a lesson to be learned from that experience as well.

Today, Kim is one of the most self-confident, positive, empowered people I have ever met. She has risen meteorically through the internationally-acclaimed Toastmasters organization. She regularly speaks in front of large audiences and for a time was a stand-up comic in local DFW clubs. She has received promotions in her career and even appeared on a podcast. More importantly, we have a great time together and often stay up conversing and laughing for hours.

Kim has overcome an unusually wide variety of serious emotional traumas in her life, all while making each one a learning experience on her personal road to empowerment.

Now, in this book, Kim shares her wisdom, together with her keen wit, to have you mesmerized with her life stories, during which you will alternatively be horrified, laugh, and cry, but with each story you will learn a valuable lesson as to how to empower yourself.

While this is a book I could not put down, it is written in a format that the reader may read individual chapters at a time and the chapters are not written chronologically. Each chapter has its own lesson, so you may return time and again to the chapters which are most helpful to you.

A unique element of this book is that each chapter concludes with one question, which will prompt you to delve into your own life and to determine what action you may take to overcome your own challenges, on your own personal journey to a BETTER LIFE through EMPOWERMENT.

Liza Urso
Attorney, Mother, and Friend

To You, Reader, From The Author

Warning! This book is raw and unfiltered. It isn't for the faint of heart. It looks at some of the ugliest moments of my life – for a purpose. Many of my greatest lessons were learned during the most painful of times.

I am taking you on a journey, but not a chronological journey. This is NOT a timeline or an autobiography. This book is organized in a different way. Each chapter is a different, stand-alone story with its own lesson.

Think of me as a kind of modern day snarky, wine-loving Aesop. Each of my stories should entertain you and connect with you, but it should also leave you with a lesson.

I've prioritized the lessons I've learned from the most basic to the more refined. However, you may find that the lesson you most need is at the end of the book, or in the middle. Embrace the stories with which you most connect. Come back to them. Re-read them. This is a journey, not a destination.

I also want you to do more than just read this book. I want you to be inspired to then look back at the painful times in YOUR life. Don't shy away. Be strong. BE COURAGEOUS. Be willing to accept responsibility – and change. Because it is only then that you can take control of your life and achieve your desires. Remember though, dear fabulous divine traveler, you are not alone. We can do this together.

I hope that you laugh with me, cry with me, and journey alongside me. I hope that you can use these lessons to better your life. They are my gift to you, for they are precious to me.

Most of all, I wish for you, from the bottom of my heart, an EMPOWERED LIFE.

Acknowledgments

To the many people who brought this book to fruition, I thank you.

Mindy, Cassidy, Becky, KelLee, and Margaret, it would not be the impactful compilation that it has become without your feedback and edits. Thank you!

Michelle Debenport, thank you for the FABULOUS cover!

To all of the authors who paved the way and gave so freely of your time and expertise to help me publish this book, I want to thank you: Wayne Lewis, Robi Ley, Lauren Midgley, KelLee Parr, Kelley Rene, and Iveth Valera.

To all of the many people who show up in these stories, thank you for being a part of my life and my story. I would not change a thing.

To everyone in Toastmasters who listened to my speeches, helped me refine my stories, and ultimately, gave me the confidence to write this book, I thank you.

To my godmother, Liza, thank you for all of your support through-out the years. You have been my second mom and I am truly grateful for you. You are wise and caring and have always believed in me. Thank you for your part in making this book become a reality.

To my sister, Krissie, I love you.

To my father, for the book you wanted to write but never did, I hope the completion of mine honors you. I love you.

To my mom, a true hero for women, whose perseverance, loyalty, dedication and work ethic have inspired me all along the way. I love you.

To my stepson Lars, I continue to learn new lessons and become a better person because you are in my life. I love you.

To Chris, the love of my life and the man of my dreams. You are my happily ever after. Thank you for giving me the gift of family. Thank you for being my companion and partner. This book wouldn't be the same without your part in it. I love you with all my heart and know without a doubt, we're so lucky.

Taking Down Walls

Everyone has a need to belong
A yearning, a passion, a feeling so strong
It hurts to be alone
It's a scar that can't be atoned
We all need people to be there
But it's so hard and we're all so scared
Of letting our true feelings show
'Cause what if someone doesn't understand or know?
We all use different methods of disguise
Whether fake happiness, intimidation, or lies
Setting up walls, a mask, or hiding behind dreams
So none of us is truly what we seem
To be at a first glance
It's not until we're given a chance
That we can tear down these walls
Let our feelings show, one and all
It takes time and we go very slow
But in time, others get to know
The real person, behind the mask
The one that cries, smiles, hurts, and laughs
We tell our secrets and learn to trust
A bond is formed that cannot bust
Everyone has a need to belong
A yearning, a passion, a feeling so strong

Kim Story, 10th Grade

Table of Contents

~1~

If Anyone Ever Knew You

2008–2009

I'm beginning my story in the middle. It's not really the middle, because in many ways, it is the beginning. I'm beginning with my bottom, my lowest point. I consider it my starting point. As cliché as it may sound, I had to lose myself before I could begin the journey of finding myself.

I'll be sharing with you the awful night I realized that I was living in a Lifetime movie. But first, a little backstory.

I was 26. I had met my boyfriend on Myspace and we bonded over our shared love of soccer. He was talented and uber confident. He very quickly introduced me to his 2-year-old son and pretty much moved himself into my apartment. The relationship moved so quickly and, even now, I don't really know exactly how it happened. Even though we had only been on one or two dates, he started asking me very personal questions about my past and my finances. I didn't want to answer them, so I lied. I lied about how many people I had slept with and I lied about how much money I made. You might think I was trying to impress him, but I think I was trying to protect myself from his judgment. I think, in my gut, I already knew.

I had been dating someone else when I met "Myspace Guy". He was someone who had gone to my high school and was kind, goofy, and witty. He really liked me. He told me I had the most beautiful smile and was surprised and delighted to find out that I liked to use all the different flavors of syrup at IHOP. He was also 6'6" and I was 5'1". He was the guy who, one day, while we were smoking a cigarette on the patio and watching the sun rise, looked over at me excitedly and said, "Kim, I've figured it out! I'm uppercase and you're lowercase!" He really did have the best sense of humor.

"Uppercase" had invited me to a lake house with his friends, and I had wanted to go with him and break it off with Myspace Guy. I don't remember what happened but Myspace Guy forbid me to go, convinced me to stay, and I canceled on Uppercase. That was one of the worst decisions of my life.

After that, Myspace Guy became my boyfriend. He bought me expensive things, like a Coach purse and Predator soccer cleats. It was different from other relationships I had had. It was so intense. I've blocked a lot of the details from that time period, but I remember a few things. He would give to get. I remember how bad I felt about myself, all the time. I remember that he would coerce me to do things sexually that I didn't want to do. I remember that once he found out about one of my lies, he started digging into all of my other lies. He found out I didn't really make as much money as I had said and I didn't think it was a big deal, but he chastised me for all of the poor financial decisions that I had made in my early 20's. He was obsessive about finding out how many people I had slept with and details about my sexual past. Looking back now, I realize that what he created in me was shame. Shame became the tool through which he would control

2

me, would control everything. Shame is the most effective tool of the dominator.

He had not been to college, so he very quickly made it a point that it was when I was in college that I had become a whore. He told me that I wasn't allowed to talk to anyone that I had met in college. He told me I wasn't allowed to talk to other guys. He told me I wasn't allowed to talk to anyone that I used to go to bars and drink with. He completely diminished my academic successes. My degree was no longer a symbol of intelligence, persistence, and pride, but rather a symbol of shame and regret. I felt so small. I felt so alone. I felt like my whole life had been a waste and I began to despair.

He got on my computer and looked at all the photos that I had stored there. Some were from high school. Some from college. Some were of ex-boyfriends. I remember the day that he hit the DELETE button. He saw the look of sadness and shock and horror on my face, and he laughed. Every single photo, every happy memory – gone in an instant – and he laughed.

He made me prove my love to him. Not just the things I had to do sexually, some of which were painful (and he delighted in my pain because my pain was proof of my love), but other sacrifices as well. I threw away all of the clothes in my closet. Thousands of dollars of clothes that I had acquired in my late teens and early 20's. Clothes that I had shopped for and paid for. Clothes that made me feel good about myself and my body. *(It's 14 years later and I am just now starting to get that feeling back, the feeling of loving my clothes and feeling good and trendy and happy when I wear them).* I threw away all of my clothes because I was such a whore that he didn't want anything from my past to invade OUR present.

I even threw away my college diploma. I took it down from my wall, exited my apartment, and walked the 30 meters to the dumpster, hesitated, then tossed it in. There wasn't anything left of me inside my body anymore and I had no will to fight the unending shame, the relentless assault upon my self-esteem.

3

At his behest, I threw away the symbol of one of my greatest accomplishments up to that point in my life. *(Thankfully, some part of Myspace Guy's conscience kicked in and he did in fact rescue my diploma – and the beautiful frame it was in – from the dumpster. To this day there is still a dent in the frame where it hit the dumpster when I dropped it.)*

I remember crying. I cried so much. I cried every day, great heaving, coughing, ugly cries. And there was no one to comfort me.

He told me he loved me. And he told me that his son loved me. He told me we would have a future together. He told me I couldn't leave him because I would be hurting his son. And he was right. I couldn't hurt his son. So I stayed. Miserable and sad and alone and hurting. Hating him and having to prove to him every day how much I loved him.

He told me he loved me and then used every awful, shameful thing I had done up to that point in my life to keep me from leaving. He told me *if anyone ever knew me, no one would love me.* I believed him. I remember thinking about all the Lifetime movies I'd ever seen and how I now understood how it happened. I was in it. I was in an abusive relationship and I couldn't escape.

Now, my lowest, lowest point. I don't remember which one of my transgressions had upset him. I'm assuming it had something to do with my sexual history. But I remember that he said I deserved to be hurt. To be hit. He told me I needed to hit myself. I was incredulous. But he meant it. So I did it. I slapped my own face. But I didn't do it hard enough. He said I needed to hit myself harder. That my first hit was weak. So I slapped myself again, hard. I burst a blood vessel in my cheek and it still shows to this day. His reaction, "Oh Kim, you hit yourself too hard! You didn't have to do that. Wow. Damn, you burst a blood vessel!"

I was stuck in the Goldilocks circle of hell, where nothing was ever "Just Right."

I was with him for almost a year and a half. I tried to leave him more than once. One of the times I tried to leave, he brought out a gun and threatened to shoot himself in front of me. He

4

said it would be my fault that his son didn't have a father. So I begged him back and we cried together and had miserable, awful, shameful make-up sex.

I wouldn't have been able to leave for good without my mom. Myspace Guy didn't allow me to talk on the phone or go anywhere without him. I never had any privacy, because a liar like me didn't deserve privacy. I had finally gotten to the point where I was so miserable that I was either going to kill myself or leave. I disobeyed Myspace Guy and went to Vista Ridge Mall in Lewisville after work and called my mom. I cried and told her I needed to leave and I needed help. My mom and I made arrangements.

I told my boss at work what I was going to do and he gave me the next day off. My boss had been so irritated by the fact that Myspace Guy kept me on the phone all day at work, nonstop, every day. Myspace Guy even accused me of sleeping with my boss after I received a $100 bonus. The only reason I kept my job was because my boss was a nice guy. He was afraid of what would happen to me if he fired me and I became financially dependent on Myspace Guy. I was afraid of that too.

On THE BIG DAY, I left for work before Myspace Guy, like I always did. But I only drove down the street to the Kroger parking lot and waited for Myspace Guy to leave. After he left, my stepdad and one of his friends helped me move what few belongings I could take into my mom's storage unit. My stepdad was my hero that day. I couldn't have done it without him.

I am so grateful that I was able to leave when so many women aren't. I'm so grateful that even after being estranged for a year, my mom still came to my rescue.

For more information about how I was able to leave this abusive relationship, go to www.fuckuptofabulous.com/freedom and download the free pdf How I Left.

Lesson #1: Trust your intuition.

You may be thinking that the lesson here is to Know Your Worth, and certainly, that is important.

But first and foremost, trust your intuition. I KNEW something was wrong from the very beginning, but I ignored that feeling. Every time I have ignored my intuition, it has gone poorly for me.

Your mind and your gut work together to protect you from danger. They can pick up on the "vibes" of a situation and person. Our eyes and ears are not as trustworthy as our intuition. I think that we, as women, have such an advantage here. Why would they call it "woman's intuition" if we were not already predisposed to be in tune with this sixth sense?

Your intuition is powerful. It gives you insight and ideas that move you toward the positive in your life. It alerts you to potential negative outcomes that you would like to avoid. You can and should TRUST YOURSELF. You are a piece of the divine, with an essence that is connected to the eternal, whether you feel it or not, it is true. You are more powerful than you know. Trust your gut.

The ideas of Know Your Worth and Know What You Want directly follow from this first lesson. To Know Your Worth is to have the strength to act on the insights your intuition provides. To Know What You Want means that you deliberately and purposefully direct your life to be in keeping with your heart's desires.

It may seem like such an obvious thing, to know what you want. Who doesn't know what they want?

As it turns out, a lot of people. One of those people was me. In my 20s I was drifting and drinking. I wanted love and a relationship, but I was directionless and desperate and needy.

I took the leftovers of whatever life was willing to give me. I didn't know my worth. I had succumbed to the victim mentality. Everything that was wrong in my life was someone else's fault (mostly my parents). I was jealous of everything that everyone else had and felt like life wasn't fair. And yet, I was still smart and pious and judgmental and unwilling to change myself.

It is no surprise that Myspace Guy found me. I didn't know what I wanted and he was someone who was more than willing to tell me what to want. I didn't know my worth, and therefore, out of a lack of trust and confidence in myself, I ignored my intuition which was all along telling me I deserved better and to avoid what was coming.

It was not an easy lesson. That was a sad, difficult, lonely, and miserable time. It took me a long time to heal from the wounds I received during that period. But I am so grateful. Since then, I have been able to focus on what I want. I have complete clarity about what I don't want and I have made it an everyday practice to contemplate what I really want out of life. I know my worth and I have confidence to trust myself. I believe in my power and let my intuition guide me, even when others question it.

So, my dear fabulous divine traveler, what is your intuition telling you?

~2~

I'm Calling the Police

1990–1996

WHAM!

A door slammed shut. Behind the door, there were still the sounds of shouting. I crouched alone in my pink nightgown, halfway up the curved staircase of our two-story home, and I could hear my parents fighting – again.

My parents didn't know that I was awake or that I was listening. I don't know why I listened. Why I got out of bed during the night to listen to them fight. Even at seven years old I was a little masochistic. It made me scared and sad, but I listened anyway. My sister slept through it all, thankfully.

I grew up with a confusing set of messages. Dad often said Mom was his best friend. He had fallen desperately in love with her, her green eyes, and her gorgeous dark hair that was so long it reached her waist. Yet, I don't remember a time when they didn't fight. I don't remember a time together that wasn't ugly. Is this what it means to marry your best friend?

9

We should have been happy. Dad was a prominent and wealthy commercial real estate attorney. We lived in a huge five-bedroom, two-story house in Dallas that was replete with a swimming pool and hot tub. Mom didn't have to work and drove me to and from the small private school that I attended until second grade. She was the ultimate chauffeur, taking me to ballet, Girl Scouts, and soccer practice. I had birthday parties with clowns and balloon animals or at theme parks where I spun around in teacups until I turned green.

But there was still the fighting. I don't remember at what age Dad told me that he and Mom never fought until I was born, but hearing that certainly left an indelible impact on me. I had never known my parents not to fight. It was my reality. But a reality I couldn't talk about. We had an image to keep up and when I talked about things that happened at home to other people, I got in trouble. I learned to keep secrets. Keep it all to myself. And I learned to listen.

Dad could be great. To our delight, he would play "airplane" with my sister and me, tossing us onto the spacious California King bed where we would bounce and giggle. He brought us treats like Mountain Dew 2-liters or Mr. Goodbar chocolate bars when he stopped by the convenience store for beer on the way home.

I remember trying so hard to prove to him that we did love him. But he would tell my sister and me, "I love you, but I know you don't love me." And we would reply, "Oh Daddy, Daddy, we do love you." It was never enough.

Dad drank beer and Mom drank wine. Mom would get tipsy and Dad would get angry. I was scared of him, especially when he yelled at us, and I could tell my mom was too.

I think I was about eight years old the first time they made me choose.

We were supposed to leave to go on vacation the next day when they started fighting that night. They stood on each side of the short end of our kitchen, maybe ten feet apart with my sister and me in the middle.

They. Made. Us. Choose. Who were we going to stay with? Dad or Mom. One or the other. We had to choose. (Not that my parents were leaving each other and we had to choose where to live. They would stay together, but we would always, daily, be choosing, one or the other).

We looked at each of them and my sister looked at me. If I was 8, then she was 5, even more terrified and confused than me. How did this happen? Why was this happening? How could I choose?

Time slowed. It was probably only five seconds but it felt like an eternity to me — the little girl and big sister who had to choose. I had to choose a parent, but my little sister chose me.

So, I did. I chose Mom. She always seemed to need me more than my dad. I felt protective of her and scared of him, so I chose her — and my sister followed. The three of us got in the van and left.

But we came back. We always came back. My parents would fight but Mom wouldn't ever leave. Dad would walk out too sometimes to go to a bar or to go to Shreveport and gamble for a few days. But he would always come back.

Years passed. The real estate market crashed, and we went from being wealthy to being not wealthy. We moved into a smaller rental house and I heard my parents frequently fight about money.

I was in seventh grade the first time Dad hurt me. In his defense, it was an accident. He and Mom were fighting again. He was angry in the kitchen and started grabbing anything within reach and throwing it at my mom. His aim wasn't great, so when he threw a plastic spatula at her, it missed and sliced a small spot on my forehead. Mom rushed from the room and hid in the master bathroom. He picked up the spatula and chased after her. I followed and watched him beat her over the head until the softer spatula part broke off and only the handle remained. He kept hitting her anyway. This is when I realized I had blood on my face. I ran to my room to look at myself in the mirror over my dresser. There was about a ½ inch cut with blood dripping out of it. Dad followed me and said he was sorry, that he hadn't been aiming for me. I started crying and asked if I would need stitches. He just sneered and laughed at me, saying, "No, it's not a bad cut" and walked away.

I told a classmate about it and she said to go to the school counselor. I did and they ended up calling Child Protective Services (CPS).

CPS decided they weren't going to take us away from my parents and I didn't want them to. My getting them involved made Dad angry and resentful and snarky though. We told him a teacher noticed the cut on my forehead and that's how CPS got involved, but he didn't believe it. He knew it was me. I had tattled on him. While he didn't hurt me because of it, the never-ending sarcasm and disdain that I experienced turned my life into a gray, numb, shadowy black hole. I was bullied, mocked, and made fun of at school and experienced a lot of the same when I got home. I wanted to die. This was the first time I started thinking suicidal thoughts. I cried myself to sleep every night thinking that no one would even notice if I was gone.

It was a year later, when I was in eighth grade, that my parents got into another intense fight. My dad liked to grab Mom by the hair and pull her around the house, which he did that night. Mom screamed and my sister cried. Then he started to choke Mom and I was truly frightened.

So I called 9-1-1.

Dad walked in while I was still on the phone. In a voice dripping with sarcasm he queried, "Oh, who'd you call this time?" The question hung in the air between us; it felt palpable. With a level of drama only available to a 13-year-old girl I retorted, "I'm calling the police!"

He started begging and telling me I shouldn't have done that. But it was too late.

Everyone had cooled off by the time the police officers arrived, but, after getting my statement and shining a flashlight on mom's raw, red neck, they cuffed Dad and led him away.

The next day my mom, sister, and I drove to Tennessee. We stayed with my grandparents for a week until Mom was ready to come back home. Dad was bailed out by then and my parents separated for a while.

After we got back from Tennessee, Mom started on Nicorette. In three weeks, she quit smoking. That week, when I was in eighth grade, was also the week Mom made a decision. She quit drinking. Now, she has been sober for over 25 years.

Lesson #2: It's never too late to change.

This story may be embarrassing for Mom because it was an awful time for her and I know she would like to forget it. It wasn't the highlight of my life either.

But I share this story with you for a reason. You need to know that you can change. You need to know that it is NEVER too late to change. If my mom could do it, you can do it.

Now, let me make this very clear to you. YOU. CANNOT. CHANGE. PEOPLE. As women, we often make the mistake of hearing the message, "It's never too late to change" and hear that as "Yes! This toxic man in my life, I can change him!"

YOU. CANNOT. CHANGE. HIM.

But you…it's never too late for YOU to change yourself for the better. My mom is A HERO FOR WOMEN. It took time and she didn't divorce Dad until many years later, but SHE CHANGED.

She went from being a stay-at-home mom who was out of the workforce, financially dependent on her husband, and emotionally dependent on alcohol, to a successful professional and a national triathlete! How much courage does that take? What mirror did she hold up to herself that week in Tennessee all those years ago? What level of love did she have for my sister and me to do *what was in her power* to be a better mom and person?

The first thing she did was to make a decision. She chose to give up alcohol and quit smoking. She chose better for herself. Getting sober was the first step for her. Then, she found a temp job as an accountant. It wasn't her dream job, but it was the first step toward financial independence. At work, she discovered she was good at what she did. She showed up and showed up and showed up. She showed up early, often arriving at work by 7 a.m. She focused on those things that were within her control. She said, "Yes," to new assignments, even when they weren't ideal and found that she became so valuable to the temp agency that they hired her on full-time, with benefits. Her confidence and finances grew and she started to have hobbies again. She joined a women's group that went on camping trips. She started to travel and have friends. She found a church community and a Bible Study group, discovering people she could trust who lifted her up and supported her as she made these positive changes in her life. She chose to change, and then she did.

Dad never changed. There will be more about him later. He died of cirrhosis, unable to quit drinking even when he knew it was killing him. Mom though…she has been my inspiration and proof that if you have courage and persistence, you CAN change your life for the better.

So, my dear fabulous divine traveler, what would you like to change?

~3~

My Greatest Disappointment

2000–2004

I loved, still love, my sister. She's three years younger than I am, almost exactly. While I grew up a nerdy, awkward, knobby-kneed tomboy with a short side-over haircut that almost exactly matched my dad's, my sister couldn't have been more different. She was an adorable blonde with a smile that was precious and infectious. People seemed drawn to love her. I would get jealous because when we would go visit my cousins in Tennessee and I struggled to fit in, they would fight over who got to hold my sister.

She had "street smarts" where I was all "book smarts." As she grew up, she made friends easily. She may have even had her first boyfriend before I did. There was a time when I was being bullied in middle school that I would hang out with her and her friends because they thought I was cool (and my peers did not).

Socializing seemed so easy for her. And God, she was so funny! Some of the most ridiculous things would happen to her and we would just laugh. She was witty, creative, and had great

15

timing with her punchlines. She excelled in art where I was better at writing. Once she was old enough, she started making her own Halloween costumes. One year she was a hobo with a torn shirt that said "California or Bust," wearing ripped jeans with hand-made grass stains, dirt on her face, and a walking stick with a red handkerchief at the end. A year later, she was a rock star in a long straight, silver-sequined dress she had made herself with material from Walmart®. Her long blonde hair was in glittery braids with a white feather boa wrapped around her bare shoulders.

Her freshman year, she chose the cheerleading path – not a surprise. She was 5'1" and 95 lbs. We were both in gymnastics, but she was the superior gymnast. While I struggled with a round-off back-handspring (and a lot of running for momentum), she could do standing flips and handsprings and had a flexibility to her body that was almost unnatural.

She also had amazing taste in clothes. The outfits she would choose to adorn her petite frame were nothing short of spectacular. Needless to say, she was in the popular crowd. (By the time I graduated high school my biggest win was simply that I wasn't getting bullied anymore.) She was beautiful and my senior guy friends would ask me if I could introduce them. (But what about me? I'm on the debate team. That's sexy, right?)

Unfortunately, my sister ended up falling into the wrong crowd. When I was away for my freshman year at Texas A&M University, my sister took her recreational drug use to the next level. She went from smoking weed and "waking 'n' baking" and graduated to crystal meth. I don't know everything that happened because I wasn't there, but I can say the decline was rapid. Within a year, the little girl that I knew and loved was gone. Oh, physically she is still here, alive to this day, but she hasn't been the same person since 2001.

She lost weight, which was scary considering she was already under 100 lbs. She started stealing – and pawning. When I came home at Christmas after my first semester in college I was going to take my bicycle back with me, but it was already gone. Jewelry, money, I don't even know all the things that went missing that year.

She transferred to an alternative school that year, and then she dropped out completely. My baby sister never graduated high school or even obtained her GED (General Education Diploma).

By my third year of college, Mom had purchased "The Club," a steering wheel lock because my sister had started stealing the car in the middle of the night. Mom would wake up and get ready for work, only to discover that her means of transportation was not in the driveway.

My sister would disappear for days sometimes. My parents learned their way around all the meth houses in South Dallas as, time and again, they went searching for her. I was so heartbroken and helpless that I told my parents to stop giving me updates. Should I go home? Could I help? How could I help? I kept waiting for the call that my sister was dead in a ditch somewhere. I prayed and prayed to God that whatever punishment and pain he had relegated to her, that he would give it to me instead.

Instead of the phone calls that she was dead, I heard about the rapes. Yes, that's plural. There was the time that she took off to Oklahoma with some drug dealer and came back, broken and crying, telling me how many times she'd been raped while she was there.

There were other times, other stories of rape, as well. I don't remember all of them. I have tried very hard not to remember them. But, and it pains me to say it, I think that some of those events were considered "payment." How else does a beautiful 15-year-old girl get the drugs she wants? I think that some of those sexual encounters were probably payment. Even so, I know that she was very mishandled and roughly treated by a lot of men. Payment or not. Poor decisions or not. My heart broke every time I heard about another time that she was abused. Over 20 years later and the tears still run like rivers when I think about it. My beautiful, blue-eyed, sweet baby sister probably prostituted

17

herself for drugs. I imagine her fear and her pain, her own lack of control over the situation in which she found herself. And even though I desperately prayed with every ounce of my being to whichever deity would listen, I couldn't save her.

I couldn't protect her. And I was angry. Angry at God, angry at my parents, angry at my sister, and angry at her "friends." Even today, I am still angry and sad and mystified. I have regrets. I wish I could have changed the outcome. I would still give anything to change the past. But I can't. I can only learn from it.

It doesn't happen as often now, but there was a time when people would constantly ask me, "What happened to your sister?" and "Why did she turn out so different from you?"

There could be many answers to this question, all the little subtleties of life and genetics, but the answer to this question really comes down to a simple answer: friends.

Lesson #3: Choose your friends wisely.

We were raised in the same house with the same parents. We lived through the same circumstances and had similar opportunities. Yes, we had very different natures and that did play a role in everything, but the one stark difference, the one that created the fork in the road from which our two lives diverged, was in our choice of friends.

My friends weren't perfect. But I was in advanced classes with other college-bound students. I was on the soccer team and debate team with other kids who had goals. Later I got involved in church groups with people who were weirdos like me and I finally found acceptance.

Almost none of my friends did drugs.

The social pressure I felt among my peers was the pressure of performance. Pressure to succeed. To have good grades, to train my body to excel on the soccer field, to train my mind to compete against others at a high level in debate. I did not have pressure to do drugs because the friends I chose didn't do drugs.

If I had chosen differently and if my sister had done the same, if our circles of influence had been reversed, it might be her writing this book for you today and me living in an assisted living house for MHMR (My Health My Resources) ladies who cannot function in society.

I know I have to include the caveat that not every person who has smoked weed or even done other drugs will end up like my sister. My point isn't what a person can do or not do and still turn out successful. There are so many factors that contribute to success. However, in the case of my sister, it was her friends who were her downfall. The ones who exploited her insecurities for their own gain. My sister's best friend from that time, the one who convinced my sister to give up cheerleading and her other friends, died of a drug overdose at age 25.

My best friend from high school later became my college roommate and she graduated with honors from the Texas A&M University School of Business. We played soccer together, and if you remember the old "anti-drug" commercials, soccer was most certainly that for me. My best friend was also my confirmation sponsor when I joined the Catholic Church. She and her parents provided a place for me to stay when things weren't going great for me at home. With them I was safe. With them, I had an example of a better life.

Jim Rohn says, "You are the average of the five people you spend the most time with." Charlie "Tremendous" Jones (more about his story in the Riverdance chapter) says, "You will be the same person in five years as you are today except for the people you meet and the books you read." When I hang out with confident, happy, healthy people, I find myself becoming a confident, happy, healthy person. When I would spend time with people who didn't have the qualities I wanted, or when I accepted whichever friendships came my way without any thought to the influence they had on me, I became less.

So, my dear fabulous divine traveler, who are your friends?

~4~

Are You Insane?!

2009–2010

My finances were FUCKED!

I had $30,000 in unsecured debt, a car loan, and another $15,000 in student loans. To some of you, those numbers will sound astronomically big, and to others of you, you're thinking, "Kim, that's a Tuesday." At the time I was only making maybe $35,000 a year, so having more debt than my annual salary was not great. For me, it became this never-ending black hole of interest rates and monthly payments that loomed over me. It was an endless cycle from which I would NEVER escape. I could see no solution.

I was also embarrassed. I was way too smart to have screwed up so badly. How had I gotten here? There was no way out. The embarrassment and shame affected EVERYTHING. It affected my confidence which affected my dating and my friendships. It affected where I ate and what I did. It was awful.

Not for the first, or the last time, I started thinking about suicide. There are no do-overs in life and I was now in a dark hole from which I would never escape. Ending the shame and ending the cycle was looking really attractive.

Let me elaborate on what a ridiculous situation I was in. At one point, I had renewed with an indoor soccer team. I was told that we would be wearing the same color shirt as we had worn the previous season. Well, something happened and we had to buy new shirts. I had to have the new shirt for the first game or I couldn't play.

I don't remember why, maybe I had miscalculated or gas prices had gone up, or I was just such a screw up that I literally didn't have the $8 to buy the shirt. $8. I didn't have $8! The day of the first game, I called one of the girls on my team and told her I was running late, so could she buy a shirt for me and I would pay her back? She gave me a little pushback and said, "Why can't you just buy it when you get here, if you're already late?" I was too embarrassed to tell her the real reason why I wanted her to get the shirt for me. She reluctantly did it and had the shirt waiting for me when I arrived at the field.

I was an awful, lying, broke, fuck up.

I started to get notices from creditors. I had started to default and now I was terrified. What would happen to me? I stopped answering my phone because of all the debt collection calls. Every call from an unknown number was sent to voicemail.

In my desperation, I finally told my dad what was going on. He was a retired attorney and knew how to negotiate. He said he would call my creditors to negotiate, but he also encouraged me to think about bankruptcy.

I did consult with an attorney about bankruptcy. Did you know that bankruptcy is expensive? I was TOO BROKE TO DECLARE BANKRUPTCY. I didn't have $8 for a t-shirt. Where would I come up with $2000+ in attorney's fees?

Dad continued to negotiate on my behalf and I continued not to have any money. What is so fascinating about this time period is that I finally did just decide to declare bankruptcy. I wanted a fresh start. I wanted to be done with it and move on with my life.

I don't know if you can relate, but just the decision to declare bankruptcy opened my brain to hope. Despair had been my companion for so long and hope and I had not spoken in years.

Hope is a dangerous thing. Hope made me think crazy thoughts. It made me receptive to lessons that I hadn't paid attention to previously.

I had been listening to Kevin Trudeau's audio set "Your Wish Is Your Command" (Trudeau 2009) when I had an "AHA" moment.

I remember standing outside my car, pumping gas, calling Dad excited and rambling about how I was going to start donating $25 each month to Habitat For Humanity. "Dad, DAD! I have wanted to BE GENEROUS, but I keep putting it off. I keep saying that WHEN I have money, THEN I'll be generous. I need to be generous NOW!"

Needless to say Dad thought I was insane and reminded me incessantly that I was facing bankruptcy and in negotiations with creditors and that NOW was exactly when I should NOT start giving money away. (Also, in case you're not great with math, $25 is more than 3x the money that I DIDN'T HAVE to buy a team t-shirt. And I was GOING TO GIVE IT AWAY, EACH MONTH! TOTALLY FREAKIN' NUTS, RIGHT!?)

Lesson #4: The formula for success is Be–Do–Have.

Part of what Kevin Trudeau teaches on the "Your Wish Is Your Command" audio series is that the formula for success is BE-DO-HAVE. Like many people, up to that point, I had been living my life with a HAVE-DO-BE mindset. I also call it the "WHEN/THEN mindset."

<u>WHEN</u> I HAVE money, <u>THEN</u> I'll BE generous.

<u>WHEN</u> I HAVE a boyfriend, <u>THEN</u> I'll BE happy.

<u>WHEN</u> I lose weight, <u>THEN</u> I'll feel good about myself.

The when/then fallacy will keep you victimized and in an endless loop of unhappiness (trust me, I know).

Kevin says that when you BECOME the kind of person you want to become, then you'll DO the things that those kinds of people do, and only then will you HAVE the results you are looking for.

He states over and over again, it is most important to BE HAPPY NOW. Be happy now. Not later. Not IF something changes. Not later when some other thing has come into your life. BE HAPPY NOW!

Something about that message hit me. It struck a chord in me. I made a choice to BE GENEROUS. NOW! Not later. Even though I was barraged by creditors and facing bankruptcy, I started making monthly donations to Habitat For Humanity.

When I donated, it reminded me that as bad a situation as I was in, it could still be worse. I have always had a place to live and a roof over my head. I actually had a lot to be thankful for.

I never declared bankruptcy. It is ironic that the decision to declare bankruptcy is what gave me the mental and emotional relief that ultimately allowed me to avoid it.

For more information about how I was able to avoid bankruptcy and change my financial future, go to www.fuckuptofabulous.com/finance and download the free pdf How I Avoided Bankruptcy.

Since then, I have not had that level of money problems. While I am still not where I would like to be financially, I have come so far. I have investments. I have savings. I've added "I'm grateful I'm so rich" to my list of mantras that I repeat regularly.

This formula has played out in so many other areas of my life. My husband, my family, my career, my health. I am so thankful for all that I HAVE because of the <u>choice</u> I made about who I wanted to BECOME. I choose to BE HAPPY NOW. So, my dear fabulous divine traveler, who do you want to BE?

~5~

First Place Goes To....

1990–1991, 2014

When I was eight years old, I read the *Disney Adventures* kids magazines. In one issue, they talked about the IRONMAN triathlon competition (and the version for kids). I became enamored with triathlons. I thought, "I love to swim and I ride my bike all the time. My only issue would be the running, but I play soccer and I'm pretty active. I think I can do this."

I did.

It wasn't the IRONMAN, but it WAS a triathlon for kids. Two years in a row, I competed in a local triathlon in Dallas. I swam, I rode my bike, I ran, and I came in second place in my age group both years. Not too shabby!

Many, many, many years later, I saw a post about the Bucket List triathlon that was hosted by the Aggie Tri group in College Station. It is a short triathlon, even shorter than a sprint. I thought that it would be a great opportunity to have an excuse to visit A&M and to get back into triathlons. I called Mom and told her

27

how excited I was. Somehow, my enthusiasm must have rubbed off on her because she decided to do it with me! 65 years old and she was going to do her FIRST EVER TRIATHLON!

About two weeks before the triathlon, I rolled my ankle playing soccer. I was incredibly disappointed that I wouldn□ t be able to compete in the Bucket List, but I still went to support Mom and my former fiancé (FF, more about him later), who had also signed up to do it with me.

The day of the race, Mom and FF both gave it their all. I was so proud of them and cheered from the sidelines. Neither of them was doing it to get a trophy. They were just excited to have completed the event and earn a finisher's medal.

But afterwards we did stick around for the awards ceremony. In category after category, "3rd place, 2nd place, 1st place. 3rd place, 2nd place, 1st place…."

Then they got to the women's 65+ category. "First place goes to Joy Story!" I couldn't have been more proud or excited as Mom walked up to receive her trophy, alone. She had been the only competitor in that category. That moment, more than any other, illuminates the next lesson.

Lesson #5: 90% of success is showing up.

This lesson isn't new or earth-shattering. It has been stated in many ways by many authors. But I still don't think it can be overstated.

Mom won that day because she showed up. No other women in her age group even attempted to do what my mom accomplished that day.

What is so amazing about my mom is that **she kept showing up.** Again and again. She has since competed – and placed – at the national level in Olympic-distance triathlons. Whatever you want in life, you can have if you just show up.

Want a paycheck? Show up for work.

Want to be healthier? Show up to the gym.

Want to be more spiritual? Show up to church.

Want more friends? Show up when invited.

Want a new job? Show up for the interview.

Want to find a relationship? Show up for the date.

The list goes on and on.

This hasn't just been true for my mom; it has certainly been true in my life as well. Showing up to networking events has allowed me to meet pivotal people who have been key to my success and progress over the last decade. Whatever you want you can have if you keep showing up to the places where those goals have a chance of coming to fruition.

So, my dear fabulous divine traveler, where do you need to show up?

~6~

I'm So Fascinated

July 2011

I looked around the cold cell. The stone walls. The bunk beds. The toilet that did not offer any privacy. I shivered. It being July in Texas, I had not worn the appropriate attire for my time in jail. The tank top, shorts, and flip flops were great when combating the death rays coming from the hellish sun, but were insufficient for my current circumstance. I took a pause, leaned back against the cold wall, laughed, then said to myself, "I'm so fascinated."

Six Months Before

Like so many people, when I was broke (broken and poor) I turned to network marketing to help improve my circumstances. In this case, my MLM of choice was Mary Kay. I was attending one of our Tuesday night team meetings – this was before Zoom, you know, when people still met in person – and the training tonight was about the power of self-talk. My director, Amber, gave us a whole list of alternative options for common, negative phrases for us to practice using. Instead of saying to ourselves, "I'm tired" or "I'm stressed," we were to use more positive alternatives. I think you see where this is going. I still remember clearly and vividly the moment when we were going through the list and Amber taught, "instead of saying 'I'm so frustrated,' you can say 'I'm so fascinated.'"

Sitting in a jail cell in Carrollton, Texas, after being picked up by a state trooper who ran my plates while I was driving back to work after lunch, I didn't feel particularly fascinated. I was fucking frustrated. I was ashamed that I had been too poor to pay that traffic ticket. I was angry that the ticket had turned into a warrant that I still couldn't afford to pay. I couldn't believe my bad luck. I hadn't been doing anything wrong that day, just driving back to work from lunch, but the state trooper ran my plates, saw the warrant, and took me in.

Now, I was cold, I was worried about what my boss thought when I didn't return from lunch, and I was kicking myself for not writing down more phone numbers before my phone was taken from me. I am a well-educated person, straight-A student and college graduate, but at no time in my life had anyone told me that cell phones don't accept collect calls (like the type of calls you have to make from jail). I had written down my mother's number and my boyfriend's number and that was it. I had optimistically (naively) thought that those two numbers would be sufficient. I was wrong. At least I had nothing but time in order to sit there and think about all of the idiotic choices I had made that landed me exactly where I was at that moment. I was well into a good bout of self-loathing and psychological self-flagellation when I mentally shouted, "This is so frustrating!" My brain immediately responded in Amber's voice, "No, this is so fascinating!"

In that moment, my sense of humor came back. I started to think about all my favorite people who had been to jail – Henry David Thoreau, Martin Luther King, ...Martha Stewart. (Some of them subscribed to civil disobedience and one of them was just disobedient). Really, if you think about it, I was in good company. And if I took a step back from myself and looked at the situation more objectively, it WAS fascinating.

I didn't have control over my circumstances in that moment. I didn't have any control over when I would be released. But I did have control over my thoughts and my words. I was still alive, I was healthy, and this situation would not last forever. If I could get control of my thinking, I could find a solution. If only I could remember someone else's number.

There was ONE number I had memorized. I gave it out on client voicemails 50 times a day. Yep, you guessed it – my work phone number.

The next time I was allowed to use the payphone, I called my work collect and left a voicemail telling my boss to let Mom know what had happened so she could help me.

My boss did even better. He gathered the $300 bail money in cash, drove to the jail, and had me released. Now, at that point, as Ricky would say to Lucy on the *I Love Lucy* show, I "had some 'splaining to do." I told my boss the story of how I ended up in that predicament and he then allowed me to pay him back by docking my paycheck in small amounts over the next two months.

Lesson #6 Change your words, change your life.

When I look back at that day, I am fascinated. Something that was such a big, frightening ordeal at the time is now barely a blip on my radar. The lesson that was ingrained in me that day has, however, remained.

Since then, my negative self-talk that used to include phrases such as "I'm fat, I'm ugly, and I have no friends" has been replaced with a new mantra: "Everything always works out for me." Just like when I was sitting in that north Texas cell, I have continued to make a habit of analyzing my words and choosing new ones. Words are powerful. Choose them wisely.

I have many mantras now. Money comes easily and frequently. I am loved and appreciated. I am a wealthy, attractive, funny, Adventurer-Teacher.

I found some of mine, but you can create your own! It is so much fun!

Mike Dooley says that "Thoughts become things," the Bible says, "Ask and it shall be given," and Pearl Strachan Hurd says, "Handle them carefully, for words have more power than atom bombs." You know this to be true. If you want to change your life, begin by changing your words.

So, my dear fabulous divine traveler, which words do you choose?

~7~

I'm Just Lucky To Be Alive

October 27, 2011

When I was poor, I had a bad habit of running out of gas in my car. Some of it had to do with money, some of it was laziness, but maybe it was that I was metaphorically always running on empty in all areas of my life and that spilled over into fueling my car. Maybe it was just that I was commuting all over DFW to get from home to work to tutoring to soccer and everything else in between. Whatever the reason, it happened, more often than I care to admit. One time happened to be MUCH more memorable than the others.

On this particular October evening, I was running late to an indoor soccer game when the light came on my dashboard, signaling that I was low on fuel. Since I was already late and driving from far away, I didn't stop to fuel up before my game. We played, we had fun, and then I returned to my car. Damn it, the fuel light was still on! I would have to stop on my way home.

35

That's okay. There was a QT a few miles up the road, right before I had to get on the highway. I could totally make it there.

I did NOT make it there.

About ¾ of a mile from the gas station, my car stopped. I wasn☐t even able to pull into a parking lot. It just stopped in the right lane of the three lanes of Southlake Boulevard as I was headed to 114. Inconvenient, but not the worst thing that has happened to me. I'm an athlete who just got done sweating and running. I could walk to the gas station and bring back enough fuel to get there and fill up the tank more completely. I was a little concerned, but I didn't panic. I turned on my hazard lights, got out of my car, and started walking. By now it was about 8:30 or 9 p.m. and dark, but I was okay.

I arrived at QT, bought a red gas can, put some fuel in it, and headed back to my car.

I watched from a distance as each step brought me closer to the blinking hazards of my stalled car. Thankfully, the tank was on the right side of the car, so I was able to stand on the sidewalk side of the street as I opened the gas cap and tilted the gas can hose into the hole. No problem.

WHAM! CRUNCH! THWAK! SCREECH!

The gas can was RIPPED from my hand and I fell back or jumped back or was pushed back, I don't know. In the spot where my vehicle had stood, a stranger's now took its place. I looked in dismay to see that my car was a good 15 feet in front of me, trunk folded in on itself, and license plate lying crunched on the street, gleaming in the moonlight.

Shock made those seconds turn into an eternity.

What? How? What? Why? Am I okay? What now? Is SHE okay?

The airbags had deployed on the sedan in front of me and I saw that a woman was sitting in the driver seat.

Time resumed its normal pace. In fact, it all became a blur.

She hadn't seen my hazards. I don't know if she was on her phone or just not looking, but she hadn't seen me and she hadn't seen my car. She rear-ended my Saturn Ion at 40 or so mph. She never even hit her brakes.

I could have been a pancake.

That was my first thought.

I'm so thankful to be alive. That was my second thought. All those months and years of gratitude training culminated into this ONE, POIGNANT, MOMENT.

Lesson #7: Be grateful, in ALL circumstances.

Years later I would attend a conference and a keynote speaker would do a demonstration with a sponge. He would tell us that we each absorb what is around us until that moment when we get "The Squeeze" put on us. The Squeeze happens to all of us, and it's when you find out if you've been absorbing the right stuff.

That night, October 27, 2011, I had "The Squeeze" put on me. For all of my stupid fuck-ups and missed opportunities and inability to even put fuel in my vehicle, in that moment, I oozed gratitude. There was a little anger there, some confusion, some disbelief, but at the core of my being it was there: Gratitude. I was thankful to be alive.

I had practiced gratitude in my everyday life to the point that in one of my hardest and scariest moments it actually became reflexive.

I'm thankful to be alive.

Even though my car was totaled and I had literally just paid it off *earlier that week*, I remained in a state of gratitude. I believe that my attitude of gratitude defined everything that came after.

Prior to that night, I had never been to a chiropractor or a masseuse.

Because of that night, a friend reached out to me on Facebook to see if I was ok. I ended up telling him about my desire to go to a masseuse. He introduced me to a friend of his, who ended up giving me free massages in exchange for tutoring services for her daughter.

Because of that night – and my minor whiplash injuries – I was able to go to a chiropractor and it was all paid for by insurance.

Prior to that night, the CD player in my car had broken and I couldn't afford to fix it.

Because of that night, the insurance company gave me a check for my totaled car. I used that check to purchase my mom's vehicle, which was newer…and had a working CD player. Because of the accident, I could now listen to personal development audio CD's while traveling to my tutoring jobs.

There were many wins that came from that terrifying night. I know that I am so blessed and so lucky. But I also know that it was the many teachers who had shared the importance of gratitude, in all situations, that allowed me to accept – and create – the blessings that came from that event.

Since 2011, I have expanded my knowledge and practice of gratitude. On January 1, 2016, I started keeping a gratitude journal. Writing down gratitudes is one of THE MOST POWERFUL actions you can take to start attracting your desires into your life. I recommend writing down at least three things you are grateful for each day. I recommend doing this first thing in the morning, to start your day focused on that for which you are thankful.

Another gratitude practice I have adopted is to think of three things I'm grateful for each night before I go to bed. Whatever you think about before you go to sleep is what your mind will dwell on in your subconscious. Program your brain for gratitude. You can also help your partner program his/her brain for gratitude by asking "What are three things you're thankful for?" before you go to sleep.

My favorite mantra that I repeat to myself in every situation in which I might feel an emotion other than gratitude is, "I'm grateful, I'm thankful, I'm appreciative." If I get stuck in traffic on the way to work it looks something like this:

> *"I'm grateful, I'm thankful, I'm appreciative. I'm grateful*
> *I have a job to drive to. I'm thankful I have a car to drive*
> *in. I'm extremely appreciative that I'm not the one who*
> *was in a wreck just now."*

This mantra and this mental methodology can be applied to ANY SITUATION. Gratitude is a habit and this is an exercise. Make your appreciation muscles strong.

Mike Dooley, contributing author of *The Secret* who coined the phrase "Thoughts Become Things," says that he and his brother will practice gratitude for things that have not yet happened AS IF THEY ALREADY HAD.

I have termed this "Gratitude 2.0 – being grateful BEFORE." In my gratitude journal, I can flip back to dates when I was grateful for promotions, or weight loss, or relationships, BEFORE those events took place. Your brain doesn't understand time. The Law of Attraction doesn't understand time. Belief is belief. Gratitude is gratitude. A "build it and they will come" kind of belief becomes a superpower when appreciation is the driving energy.

So, my dear fabulous divine traveler, what are you grateful for?

~8~

I Love My Life!

2011

I was sitting in the nosebleed seats at my first ever Mary Kay Seminar convention. I was surrounded by other entrepreneurial women, all of us hanging on the edge of our seats, listening to top Mary Kay saleswomen inspire us with their stories and wisdom.

Then, SHE got on the stage.

I don't remember her name. But her impact has reverberated throughout the course of my life since that day.

She was a blonde ball of boundless energy and enthusiasm. Every fiber of her being was pulsing with pure joy. The pinnacle moment of her keynote was when she spread her arms wide and on a stage in front of tens of thousands of other women she shouted, "I LOVE MY LIFE!"

I thought to myself, *I love my life?* The look on my face most closely resembled Keanu Reeves in *The Matrix*: "WHOA."

It's a simple enough statement. I love my life. Simple words. Nothing particularly profound. But it shocked me to my core.

41

I had spent so much time hating myself, hating my parents, hating my circumstances, in essence, hating my life.

I started thinking. I didn't love my life. And if I was honest with myself, I didn't know anyone else who did either.

I wanted what SHE had. I wanted to feel that energy, that enthusiasm, and that certainty. What would it take for ME to love MY LIFE? What kind of person would I have to become to feel compelled to go on stage and leave every ounce of reserve behind. To open my arms and shout to the masses, "I LOVE MY LIFE!"

I'd have to be fucking crazy. But if crazy felt that good I knew I wanted it.

It was only a few months after I left that conference that I had another "WHOA" moment. I came across the following quote, "Instead of planning your next vacation, plan a life you don't need to take a vacation from."

WHOA!

What would it take to create a life I didn't need to take a vacation from?

Lesson #8: Create a vision for your dream life.

Over the last decade, I've learned a lot about vision. One of my favorite stories, and one I incorporate into a lot of my speeches on the topic, is the story of Florence Chadwick. Florence was an American swimmer who set records for long-distance swimming in the 1950s. This particular story is from when she attempted to swim the 26 miles from the California coastline to Catalina Island. She had been swimming for 15 hours when a heavy fog set in, eliminating her visibility (and her faith in her ability to complete her goal).

She swam for another hour before admitting defeat.

Once she was in the boat, she learned that she had quit **only one mile short of her goal.**

She had completed 25 of the 26 miles but had given up because she was unable to see her destination.

However, like a true champion, she trained for two more months and then attempted the 26-mile swim again.

It was the same distance. She encountered the same fog. However, this time she was SUCCESSFUL! She completed the swim.

When asked what she had done differently, she said that she kept a vision of the shoreline in her mind while she swam. During those two months of training, she had been visualizing the shore while she practiced.

What she saw in her mind's eye was the determining factor between her success and her failure. It wasn't her body, but her mind that she needed to train.

What does this mean for the rest of us?

Many successful people create vision boards. It's even one of the tips recommended in the book and movie, *The Secret*. Mike Dooley talks about having a vision notebook and in his speech "Thoughts Become Things" he details how his "WHOA" moment was sitting and looking out of a hotel on a vista that had been a picture pasted in his notebook only a year before.

I find this technique particularly successful for acquiring my physical desires. I created a vision board that became the template from which I have built not one, but two, beautiful backyard garden paradises.

It was fascinating when I discovered that the Spanish-style stucco and palm tree landscaping of the apartment I lived in for two years almost exactly matched a picture I had cut out four years before and pasted to a forgotten vision board.

Just this past year I had the opportunity to ride in an Alfa Romeo for the first time – a car that had been posted a decade before on my vision board as my dream car. I had forgotten it was there until I was already in the vehicle and realized, "Holy shit, I am right now living out a dream that I had a decade ago."

Whether you are training for a challenging goal or just wanting home décor inspo, vision is an integral step on the road to achievement. Vision boards and notebooks are tangible ways to create your dream life. Strengthen your mind's eye muscle and no goal is out of reach. You, too, CAN and SHOULD have a life you LOVE enough to stand on a stage and scream it loud for all the world to hear!

So, my dear fabulous divine traveler, what is the vision for your dream life?

~9~

The Path to Toastmasters

2010–2014

Have you ever looked back and found that although you felt lost at the time, in retrospect, everything was working out just as it should be? I hope so. I hope you can think of those examples from your life. I'm going to share one of mine.

I've already shared with you what a mess my life was in my mid-20s. It was shortly after I left my abusive ex, Myspace Guy, when I was already feeling the throes of financial distress, that I found myself over at a friend's apartment. We had known each other since our freshman year of college when we lived in the same dorm building together. We ended up taking a few classes together, going to church together, playing soccer together, and volunteering together. We graduated from college in the same year and both moved back to DFW.

She was one of the few people I was able to reconnect with after I left Myspace Guy, which is how I ended up at her apartment. I was overwhelmed and hurting and sad and stressed and feeling like a failure. I started to cry. I mean, really cry. This wasn't a *lovely cascade of tears caressing my cheeks.*

I started to cry the ugly cry. Great heaving breaths of desperation as the stinging hot torrents pouring from my corneas burned a path down my red and blotchy face. It was not my finest moment.

My friend didn't really know what to do, but since I had mentioned my money problems she asked, "Have you read *Rich Dad, Poor Dad?*" I responded that I had not and she said she had recently read it, that it was a popular finance book, and that it might be helpful for me.

THAT became one of the moments that changed my life.

Because I had been crying the ugly cry on my friend's sofa, she recommended I read *Rich Dad, Poor Dad.*

Because I read *Rich Dad, Poor Dad*, I started a Mary Kay business.

Because I started a Mary Kay business, I started networking.

Because I started networking, I met an entrepreneur named Nick.

Because I met Nick through networking, he recommended I listen to the audio "The Strangest Secret" by Earl Nightingale on YouTube.

Because I listened to "The Strangest Secret" on YouTube, YouTube generated a recommendation for a similar speech. It was Mike Dooley's speech, "Thoughts Become Things," which he was giving at a Toastmasters speech contest.

THIS became another moment that changed my life. Not only is Mike Dooley one of my favorite authors and speakers (who I had the pleasure of meeting when he was here in Dallas in 2015), but it inspired me to get involved in Toastmasters, which has since put the positive changes in my life into hyperdrive.

Kim, what is Toastmasters? I'm so glad you asked!

Toastmasters is an international organization with the mission of helping people become better communicators and leaders.

Many people will join Toastmasters to get over their fear of public speaking. However, the ancillary benefits go so much deeper than simply giving presentations. Toastmasters is a safe place to build confidence, find your voice, and take the next step to becoming the leader you were meant to be.

The Core Values on which the program is built are: Integrity, Respect, Service, and Excellence. I truly believe, with all my being, that this world needs Toastmasters. We need leaders who have integrity, who respect the dignity of every person, who believe that leadership begins with serving and meeting the needs of others, and who inspire excellence. I joke that when you start, you are getting into Toastmasters, but at some point, Toastmasters gets into you, and THEN the magic happens.

A decade ago, I was crying the ugly cry on my friend's sofa. Since then, I have been a guest speaker on the *Inspire & Empower* podcast, served as a leader to thousands of Toastmasters members in the DFW area, conducted multiple workshops on leadership and public speaking, and been sought out as a mentor. How?

Lesson #9: One step at a time.

There are many amazing quotes and adages to this effect. A few of my favorites are, "The journey of 1,000 miles begins with a single step" and "How do you eat an elephant? One bite at a time." "How do you journey from California to New York while driving in the dark? See as far as your headlights will take you, then go further. Do it again and again until you reach your destination."

I spent 15 years in the test-prep industry, helping high school students achieve their desired scores on the SAT and ACT college entrance exams. What made me an excellent teacher? My ability to help my students transform large and daunting goals into smaller, accessible pieces.

Want to achieve a 1500 on the SAT? Okay great! Do you want that to be a 750 in Math and a 750 in Verbal? 780 and 720? How many questions do we need to get correct on the math section to achieve this goal? On the verbal? How many can you miss on each section and still succeed? Where are you now and what is your practice plan to get from here to there? How much time will you dedicate to this goal each week? Which days are best? What is your level of commitment? On a scale of 1–10, how important is this 1500 to you?

These questions are very specific to my work with high school students taking the SAT, but I think the process is universal. Whatever your goal, particularly if it is large and daunting, break it into smaller, actionable pieces.

Remember though, you don't have to have ALL the steps. The lights aren't going to ALL be green when traveling from California to New York. You just have to take the first small step. Any action is action – as indicated by the action to completely lose my shit on my friend's sofa all those years ago. In many cases, any step is better than no step at all.

What are the two pieces of information that you need in order to effectively use a GPS? Your destination – AND – your starting place. If you know where you are and where you want to go and you start taking steps toward your goal, you will see progress. Progress begets more progress. Momentum speeds up. But action is the magic that makes it happen. You can have a perfectly planned route, but if you don't press the gas, you won't go anywhere.

You can go by bus or train or plane. By bike, by sled, by board. By boat or jet ski. Porsche or Jeep. Diesel or EV. So many options!

Some of those methods of transportation are more effective than others…while some are just so much more FUN! The possibilities are endless, but you have to take that first step, and keep on moving. Just one step at a time. Just imagine what you can accomplish!

So, my dear fabulous divine traveler, what's your first step?

~10~

Riverdance

November 23, 2017

It was Thanksgiving Day a few years ago. I had woken up and run the 5K Turkey Trot that morning (because apparently the way that I earn my tryptophan is to wake up before the sun rises and freeze my nonexistent balls off). Running is awful. But at least I had friends there to share in my misery. Because shared misery is still misery.

Apparently there were some endorphins firing after the 5K so I was actually in a pretty good mood as I drove the 30 minutes back to my apartment. I parked my car in the garage and walked hastily to my door, prepared to grab the ingredients for the vegetable casserole I'd be cooking later that day, feeling REALLY excited about all the food I'd be consuming.

I LOVE Thanksgiving. It's the only holiday with which I don't have traumatic memories from my childhood. It is a holiday all about food and fellowship AND it's always on a Thursday so it usually signifies a four-day weekend. It's fucking brilliant!

51

"Huh, that's odd," I said to myself, noticing the wetness on the ground as I unlocked the door.

I stepped inside the door and heard – and felt – a splash. I looked down and all around. Shock and disbelief rolled over me in waves as I assessed the situation. There was an inch or two of water over the entirety of the hardwood floors. I called my roommate, Stephanie, who, thankfully, was an employee of our apartment complex management company. I think she was also at a 5K that morning. She made some calls and was even able to get ahold of our onsite maintenance. She was a ROCKSTAR that day! But she was also distraught. Steph had bought brand new furniture when we moved in together. She was frantically trying to minimize the damage.

We found out that a pipe had burst, flooding just three of the apartments on the first floor on our side of the building. (Not sewage, thank God!)

I worked with my roommate to do what I could and when we were at a stopping point, I did what everyone should do in that situation.

I did a Riverdance in my living room. Kicking up water, arms folded, legs akimbo (and flailing).

It was hilarious. Stephanie stopped everything to get the ridiculousness on video. She laughed, I laughed, and we both relaxed. It is still one of the highlights of my life that I literally got to dance on water in my living room.

Lesson #10: Find the funny.

Back in 2006, I took a stand-up comedy class at the Addison Improv with a local comedian, Dean Lewis. Dean would always remind us to "Find The Funny." From him I learned how to take real life and real emotions and find the humor, irony, or absurd. Finding the funny was about more than puns or punchlines.

I find this lesson to be THE ONE that is the most lacking in the self-help industry. It's become my superpower over the years and I attribute a lot of my resilience in the face of challenges to this ability.

This lesson also appears in J.K. Rowling's Harry Potter series. In book 3, she introduces us to a being called a boggart. A boggart takes on the form of our greatest fear. Any idea what the spell is to overcome the boggart?

Riddikulus!

The spell "Riddikulus" transforms your greatest fear into something ridiculous. Your greatest fear is no longer frightening, but funny. How empowering is that!? How much better would our lives be if we metaphorically waved our wands and declared Riddikulus at our fears?

For more ideas on how to find humor in any situation, go to www. fuckuptofabulous.com/humor and download the free pdf Humor Is My Superpower.

I am inspired by the story of Charlie "Tremendous" Jones. Charlie was diagnosed with a terminal illness and only given months to live. The doctors gave him a ZERO percent chance of survival.

Charlie made a choice. He decided that he would laugh until he died (This is not a typo. Died, not cried). He started watching his favorite comedies. He laughed for hours on end. Months later, the miraculous happened. CHARLIE WAS CURED.

He had laughed himself back to health. ::INSERT MINDBLOWN EMOJI HERE::

Laughter is the best medicine is more than just some meaningless adage. It is true. You can read up on all the health benefits of laughter on WebMD on your own time. I'm not a scientist. But the science IS there.

As a speaker I've learned that incorporating humor into your speeches helps lower the audience's guard and creates connection. Professional speakers who are funny make more money.

But maybe you aren't a professional speaker and what I just said doesn't apply to you and your life. So what about dating websites? What's THE TOP characteristic single people are looking for in a partner's personality? A sense of humor!

My husband and I laugh together. We may not be the attractive couple or the rich couple or the (insert desirable quality here) couple. But we ARE the funny couple. My husband, my friends, my family – I keep people around me that I can laugh with.

So, my dear fabulous divine traveler, how can you find the funny in your life?

~11~

Cat Ransom

2013–2015

The year was 2013. (Apparently that was a decade ago, but I am in denial about the passage of time.) I was living with two other single ladies and we were having a pretty good time being single. We would go out for drinks and dancing and even had a local bar *where everybody knew us by name*. The week before my birthday, we went out and met a couple guys who were playing pool. I hit it off with one of them and invited him to come to the birthday party at our house that following weekend. He didn't show. Whatever, no big deal.

A month later, I stopped by the same bar on my way home from something. I don't remember why I was there alone – whether I was waiting on my girlfriends or whether my girlfriends had other plans, which is exactly why I ended up at the bar alone. Next thing I know, I see the guy from the month before at the other end of the bar. I think he smiled and waved at me and I ended up sitting next to him talking. We were laughing and having a great time, so when he invited me over to his place, I said yes.

I followed him in my own car, eyes getting wider as we turned into one of the really nice neighborhoods. I thought I had to be dreaming when he pulled into the driveway of this fantastically gorgeous two-story home.

I got out of my car and he led me inside. He gave me the tour and let me tell you, for an upper-middle class home (not mansion uber rich, but upper middle class), this home WAS GORGEOUS. I loved the cabinets, the layout, the décor, all of it was FABULOUS. I did have a moment when I was like, "Huh, why would a single guy need all this house?" but my awe squelched that question real quick.

He showed me the upstairs gameroom which was seriously badass. It had the built-in bar, a pool table, darts, and signed sports memorabilia from amazing athletes completing the look. This room opened out onto the wooden deck which had a view of a nearby lake. The weather was perfect as it often is in October and I stood out there on that deck, enjoying the breeze and the conversation. We had a couple beers and then, this guy who seemed to have everything and why on earth would he be interested in me, leaned in to kiss me.

I know you'll be totally shocked to find out I did in fact stay the night in his four-poster Tempur-Pedic bed with the sage duvet cover. I felt like I was a princess in some fairy tale and couldn't believe something so amazing was happening to me.

He had told me he had to wake up early the next morning to play golf with his father, so the next morning we woke up early and I left.

We had traded phone numbers and, good to his word, he called. The conversation didn't quite go the way I anticipated though.

"Hey Kim, good to talk to you. There's something I need to tell you. I don't know how to say this, but I'm married."

What in the ACTUAL FUCK!? To my knowledge I had never slept with a married man before, but I guess there's a first time for everything. (insert 1 million facepalm emojis here)

He continued, "I felt so bad about it I woke up sick this morning. You should know though that we are separated and we are getting a divorce, it just hasn't happened yet."

Of course I asked the question that every woman would ask next. "So do you have any kids?"

"Well, about that. That's my other complication. I do have a daughter. She's 13. But I only found out about her a couple years ago. It was a one-night stand, but her mom found me because she needed money. It's a complicated story, but her mom has three children from three different dads and my daughter thought one of them was her dad for years but now he's in prison so the mom found me. She lives about three hours away and I see her every few months."

WOW!

So, like a good, sane, rational woman, I took all these red flags I had just absorbed and decided this guy was not the guy for me.

Right?

Fuck no!

I listened to his sob stories about his soon to be ex-wife and his baby mama and ate that shit up. I mean, he had a beautiful house and was a successful businessman. He had to be a good guy, right?

We started dating and I started staying over. Within a couple months, I had even moved my cat.

That Christmas he SPOILED ME. Bought me a diamond tennis bracelet and a fancy bathrobe and I don't even remember what else. No one had ever bought me gifts like that before. I felt like I was Cinderella. I could not believe this was happening to me. All my prayers were finally being answered. It had to be love, right?

But, when we were around certain people, he would tell them we were "friends." He told me that, because of the divorce, he couldn't let people know we were together, yet. But the divorce would be over in like a month or two, so I could wait, couldn't I?

When his wife called to talk about things and it made me uncomfortable, he told me he had to talk to her and be nice to her so that the divorce would be more amicable.

He told me that he had some money problems but that they were his ex-wife's fault. He told me that she would spend money and he couldn't stop her. I believed him. He had to be telling the truth, right?

At this point I'm going to name this guy "FF." FF liked to drink and go to bars. There was one night that he went out without me. I remember I had a very bad feeling about it. He didn't want me to come up there and meet him and had one of his buddies get on the phone, laughing and saying that they were having guy time. My gut said otherwise. I'm pretty sure he cheated on me that night.

That being said, I cheated on him one night with an ex. The sex with FF was awful, had always been awful, and would continue to be awful. But I was in love with the house and the lifestyle. I would never be able to live that nice of a lifestyle on my own. I stayed. But one night I cheated. This was about six months into our relationship and on Texas Rangers baseball opening day, he asked me about the night before. I lied. I lied again. I lied again. But somehow, he knew. I'm not sure how. So, I finally told him the truth. I confessed that I had cheated on him the night before. I remember it was opening day because we were meeting friends and it was an incredibly *awkward day*.

But his divorce still wasn't final. "It will only take a month or two" turned into 13 months. Thirteen months that we dated and were "together" and he was still married to someone else. Thirteen months of wondering if he would ever be able to marry me.

This is also when I found out that for all of his "STUFF," he had no savings. During the divorce, he couldn't take on any more credit card debt, so it was actually my savings that had to pay for various things that came up unexpectedly.

About the time that he was finally divorced is also when my job had turned toxic. I wasn't appreciated and there were not any opportunities for growth. I found another job and quit. The same week I started my new job, my grandfather passed away.

As you can see, this was a confusing time for me. I wasn't happy but I was also trying to make it work. I thought if I fixed my job situation and grieved my grandfather, then everything would be better. I still thought that the issues were my fault. I also didn't know if I left if it would be any better with anyone else. So I stayed.

The next month we threw a birthday party for FF. He liked whiskey so there were whiskey tastings and as often happens with whiskey, a few people overindulged. One of my friends got drunk, got sick and threw up, and next thing I know, FF had punched him. Gave the guy a bruise under his eye. I didn't see it, because I was upstairs, but by the time I got downstairs the bruise had already appeared. That moment was the first time I was truly scared of FF. He was a big, tall, thick guy. He had seemed so gentle when we first met but the longer I knew him, the more that it seemed to be a façade.

This new job wasn't a great fit, so I found myself working for minimum wage at Calloway's Nursery while I tried to figure out if I wanted to be a nursery and landscape professional. I loved plants and had already built a beautiful garden at FF's house. Maybe this was my calling in life. But I had no money. That's okay though. FF would take care of me, right?

Somewhere about this time, we got engaged. He proposed at half time of one of our soccer games. It should have been fun and romantic, but since we had been fighting earlier that day, I think he decided to propose that night to make me feel bad for fighting. It wasn't the first time or the last time I would feel manipulated.

Weddings are interesting. You really find out about each other's values.

FF had been promising me a fairy tale wedding ever since we first got together. But the money wasn't there. We took vacations and he bought more things, but he never made it a priority to save money for a wedding.

We sent out Save The Date cards. And then, only a few months later, we let everyone know that we were postponing the wedding. I felt so embarrassed. I knew everyone must be judging me and wondering what was going on.

Six months after his divorce, and finally able to have a credit card again, FF had already racked up $10,000 in credit card debt. My unease continued to grow. Our physical relationship was never great, but I told myself we were in our 30s and maybe great sex doesn't happen after you leave your 20s. Maybe it wasn't that important.

We started fighting. One night I told him I was going to sleep in the guest bedroom instead of with him. However, when I did try to get into the master bedroom, the door was locked. I tried again. I couldn't get in. I asked him about it.

"Did you lock me out?"

"No, no I didn't. Why would you think I would do that? You're going crazy."

I was familiar enough with the idea of gaslighting to think "Whoa." It wasn't so much that he had locked me out of the bedroom as his perfect ability to lie to me about it and to turn it back on me.

I really struggled for the next couple of months. We were supposed to get married. This was supposed to be my happily ever after. It was supposed to finally be happening for me! I couldn't leave. Maybe this was the best I deserved. I couldn't afford to leave. We had moved my father into the guest bedroom, because I was tired of not knowing if he was dead or alive. Now, I couldn't leave FF AND take care of my father and myself. I was stuck. I couldn't have ANOTHER failed relationship. I would be a failure. I was a failure.

I don't know who needs to hear this, but here it is:

Lesson #11: There is life after an ending.

One night FF and I were invited to my friend Chris' house to celebrate Becky and Patrick's anniversary. That was the night I found out from one of my other friends that Chris and his wife had gotten a divorce only a few months before. I was shocked. I thought they were a great couple and were perfect for each other. They had a young son and had just recently moved into this house. What had happened? How was Chris doing? And where was Chris anyway?

Not too long after FF and I arrived at the party, Chris finally showed up – making an epic entrance into the swimming pool with a naked cannonball.

There was something about that moment, expecting to see this distraught, upset guy and instead seeing a guy who was embracing life in spite of the circumstances. It opened up my mind to the possibilities. Maybe my life wouldn't be over if I left FF. Maybe there could be happiness after.

Chris and I talked a lot that night. I was so impressed by him and his attitude. His desire to make the best of a bad situation. I wanted to be like that.

Less than six weeks later, I left FF. My dad and I found an apartment together that we could afford. I had found my dream job working full time in the test prep industry. I was truly happy. The weight of that relationship no longer weighed on me.

I think that because we as women are so relationship-oriented and even define ourselves by our relationships, that we believe ourselves to be failures if we end a relationship. I was truly terrified to leave FF. I knew I wasn't happy. I knew I was settling if I stayed with him. I knew I had begun my relationship with him for all the wrong reasons back at the beginning. But I still truly believed that I would be a failure for leaving him.

Nothing could have been further from the truth.

Having the self-respect to leave a man who didn't treat me well – he bought me things, but he didn't treat me well – made me a better person. Having the strength to do what I knew was right instead of staying because of obligations made me stronger.

I had created a prison in my mind, but when I moved out, I left those chains behind as well.

There is life after divorce. There is life after breaking off an engagement. There is life after moving out on your own.

Some of those changes may be painful or challenging, don't get me wrong. But they are not fatal.

It is better to be single than to be in a bad relationship. You spend a lot of time with a significant other.

I also think you learn more about a person from his/her reaction to a breakup than you ever learn during the relationship. If I ever had any regrets about leaving FF, they were soon dispelled.

Even while he was begging me back, I found out that he had been sleeping with other people. A random lady messaged me on FB messenger saying, "I just thought you should know." He very quickly got into another relationship and started posting about it. I wouldn't have cared, except, FF STILL HAD MY CAT!

I broke up with him in August and didn't get my cat back until DECEMBER. I had to threaten to call the police or take him to small claims court before he would finally respond. He told me that I still owed him $125 from when we had a shared phone account and he wouldn't return my cat until I paid him the money.

I met him in the parking lot of the PetSmart near his house, cash in hand, since he wouldn't accept a check, and finally did the deal and made the exchange to get my cat back.

I had to pay him Cat Ransom.

Once someone shows you who they are, believe them. I let the quality of his things and the glamor of a lifestyle blind me to the quality of his character. I spent 13 months living with a man whose divorce wasn't yet final. I got engaged to someone who never treated me like a person and who never loved me for who I was. I resigned myself to crappy sex 'til death do us part. I tried to make a relationship out of a mutual desire to own things. None of that was love.

No one judged me when I left. The people who really cared about me were happy if I was happy. They supported me. They helped me. They comforted me when I cried and kept me company when I was lonely.

I am so thankful that I realized there was life on the other side of that difficult decision. I wasn't a failure. Neither are you if you make decisions that help you to be true to yourself.

If something isn't working in your life, it is okay to walk away, whether it's relationships that aren't serving you or dead-end jobs that don't encourage growth. Life is too short not to be happy. Take courage and know that it will all work out.

So, my dear fabulous divine traveler, what do you need to walk away from?

~12~

The Nerd Chapter

Approximately 1987–Present

One of the greatest blessings in my life is that my parents instilled in me a love of reading. When I was growing up, my parents had a whole room dedicated as a library. (This is where, at the age of nine, I discovered one of my mom's romance novels. I had SO MANY QUESTIONS).

Both of my parents loved reading and loved education. My mom went back to school to get her master's degree in library science and my father graduated *cum laude* from law school. Trips to the library were the highlight of my day during the summer. I remember that the Dallas Public Libraries would do their summer reading competition and I would color in each pie piece every time I completed another 15–minute reading session – well, actually I would be coloring in whole pies after my most recent 2-hour book consumption. I ran out of tracking sheets that summer and the librarians responded, "Here, take your prize, just stop killing trees." I didn't read books, I devoured them.

When I was in fourth grade (after I had just skipped over third grade), I was still so above-level that my teacher had one competition with prizes for the rest of the class, and for me, she just promised to give me a set of her favorite books by one of her favorite authors. It turned out to be J.R.R. Tolkien's *The Hobbit* and *The Lord of the Rings*. I still have the dog-eared, torn-cover copies in my library today. When I was in tenth grade GT English, and we were studying *The Hobbit*, it was the only time in my entire high school career I had the popular girls vying with each other to be in my project group.

While other children were unable to sit still in church, my mom just handed me my copy of *Sacagawea* and I was quiet throughout the whole service. There are parents to this day that remember me as "that little girl who was always so quiet reading in church." I had the *Book of Common Prayer* memorized so I could make the necessary responses without looking away from my own novel.

When I was young, I loved books like *Island of the Blue Dolphins, Caddie Woodlawn, Dawn Rider,* and *The Secret Garden.* Books about young women who had spirit and weren't afraid to stand up and fight for that in which they believed. I had a whole section at home devoted just to Nancy Drew and the Anne of Green Gables series.

I loved fantasy and sci fi as well. If the book had a unicorn in it, it was mine. *Ender's Game* also quickly became one of my favorites.

And, of course, *Choose Your Own Adventure* could keep me occupied for hours.

Honestly, I got along better with books than people. I never felt like I fit in with my peers, but in a book, I became someone else. Or maybe, looking back, it was that I related so much to the female outcast heroines in these stories. These were the friends who understood me. I certainly understood them. I understood their loneliness. I felt the emotional turmoil. I knew what it was to be "different." I hoped that someday, like them, this would become an asset and a strength.

I don't know if I have lived up to that ideal, but I do know this. My love of reading saved me. When my life was falling apart and I didn't know what to do, I turned to books. The knowledge and wisdom of others helped me to learn from my mistakes and begin to create the fabulous life I always imagined. This, then, is the next lesson:

Lesson #12: To be empowered, be a reader.

Whether you look at the quote by Harry S. Truman, "Not all readers are leaders, but all leaders are readers," or the words from Charlie "Tremendous" Jones, "You will be the same person in five years as you are today except for the people you meet and the books you read," the message is the same – reading books is important to success.

There are some books that provide new information. They give you new facts to add to your repertoire, or they entertain you. But there is another type of book. I call this kind of book a "paradigm-shifter." You become a new person with a new outlook on life after having read this book. I very desperately wanted to share in my own book, a list of these paradigm-shifters that have changed my life for the better, and here they are.

I remember the first time I read *The Five Love Languages* (Chapman 2010). I was a senior in college and in a romantic relationship. I also still had a tumultuous relationship with my parents and with my sister. After reading *The Five Love Languages*, my life was forever changed and so many mysteries unraveled before me. My primary love language is Words of Affirmation and my secondary language is Physical Touch with Quality Time close behind. Gifts do not even register on my radar. I just consider it all "stuff." But my younger sister's love language WAS gifts. I had thought her superficial, but at her core, these "things" were how she needed to give and receive love. WHOA! My mom's primary love language is Acts of Service and conflicts we had in our past are absolutely explained when you look at them through the Acts of Service vs. Words of Affirmation frame of reference. Her feelings were hurt when I told her I didn't care if she attended my National Honor Society ceremony or when I told her that if she didn't want to do something I could just do it myself. She, on the other hand, found me to be narcissistic. Why would she tell me how great I was and give me a big head? For most of my life, my mom told everyone else how proud she was of me, but rarely ever said it to me…until *The Five Love Languages* changed our lives and our relationship.

Rich Dad, Poor Dad (Kiyosaki 1998) was another game changer for me. I had never analyzed my thoughts about money before. I had never questioned the "go to school, get a good job, buy a home, work until you retire" life plan prior to this 4-hour read. I never thought about the dichotomy of "working for money" vs. "having money work for you." I highly recommend this book as a starting point for changing how you think about money.

The one book that I listen to over and over and over again on repeat is *The 4-Hour Work Week* (Ferriss 2007). Once you have read *Rich Dad, Poor Dad* and realize that the game we are playing isn't worth winning, Tim Ferriss gives you the practical guidelines that help you realize that you can start where you are, right now, even in the job at which you are currently working, and improve your life, now. You don't have to become a real estate investor (unless you want to) to achieve the life of your dreams. You can spend more time with your family, you can travel, and you DON'T have to delay it all until you are 65.

Even if you are not Christian and don't believe in God, I still believe that *The Shack* (Young 2007) is a worthwhile read. I have never read a story that so perfectly encapsulates and explains why bad things happen to good people and how God can love us and still bad things can happen to us. It explains how we can love and forgive our neighbors, our family, and even our enemies when they do awful things. This world needs more love, more understanding, and more forgiveness, and this book shows us a path for doing just that.

I talk elsewhere about the importance of boundaries and how necessary they are for living a healthy and happy life, but I do want to recommend the book *Boundaries* (Cloud 1992). I have re-read it at different times and found new lessons that pertained to new chapters in my own life. This was monumental for me and a huge stepping stone in overcoming the victim mentality mindset that can be so easy to fall into but depressingly hard to get out of.

How To Win Friends and Influence People (Carnegie 2009) is a classic, and for good reason. Dale Carnegie turns every bad habit that we develop and challenges us to treat people better. If you only read the chapter "Don't Criticize, Condemn, or Complain," your life will already be changed for the better. I find myself repeating that chapter title as if it were a mantra: "Don't criticize, condemn, or complain, don't criticize, condemn, or complain." (My husband and stepson probably wish I was better at actually *executing* that mantra....)

I also think it's important to talk about *The Secret* (Byrne 2006). If you don't know anything about the Law of Attraction, this is the place to start. There are many authors who contributed their stories in *The Secret*, and I have delved more deeply into this topic, and recommend you do the same, but this book is an important starting point. It's the tip of the iceberg for understanding the metaphysical laws of life that surround us. Once you've read it, I encourage you to continue your own journey to get a more full picture of the entire iceberg.

If you only read these seven books: *The Five Love Languages*, *Rich Dad Poor Dad*, *The 4-Hour Work Week*, *The Shack*, *Boundaries*, *How To Win Friends and Influence People*, and *The Secret*, I truly believe that your life will be changed for the better. Well, eight books, including this one.

Even more than making specific book recommendations, the bigger point of this chapter is that reading books expands your mind. It can change your paradigm. I hope that you can find yourself open to new ways of thinking. I hope that you can keep your mind flexible. Being trapped by limiting thoughts is the opposite of empowerment. Learning from the wisdom, experience, and study of others is much easier than making all of the mistakes on your own.

So, my dear fabulous divine traveler, what do you need to read?

~13~

Farts Help My Prayer Life

2018

I stood to the side of the stage at the Toastmasters Division B Contest in Fort Worth, Texas, waiting for the Contest Master's formal introduction (Name, Speech Title, Speech Title, Name).

"Kim Story, Farts Help My Prayer Life. Farts Help My Prayer Life, Kim Story."

I shook hands with the Contest Master, crossed to the middle of the stage, looked out at the audience, pursed my lips and made the largest, longest fart noise I could make. The audience just stared at me in shock. What the hell had I just done?

I've given thousands of hours of presentations in my life. Some of them have been more difficult than others. Some of them have been more personal than others, some more inspiring.

But the most challenging that I ever wrote was for a humorous speech contest. I had progressed a lot during my previous five years in Toastmasters. I had given tear-jerker speeches about my sister. I had done a solo sketch performance of my favorite

71

scenes from Monty Python and the Holy Grail. ("It's merely a flesh wound.")

I had even performed a hilarious one-act play about a besotted young woman visiting her serial killer boyfriend in jail, ending with my strumming an invisible guitar and singing my undying love to him.

But there was one topic that was 100% taboo. Off limits. Never to be mentioned.

Farts.

I hate farts. I hate the word, the noise, the smell. I hate it all. I didn't even know they were called farts until I was in high school. My family called them booms — as in "Daddy boomed." (Daddy boomed a lot.)

My most embarrassing moments in my whole life, where I wanted the ground to rise up and eat me, all revolved around farts.

I was in fifth grade the first time my body betrayed me. I've already shared with you that I was a nerdy, socially awkward kid. I was not cool or confident. I could not just "pull it off."

We were taking a test. It was while sitting at my single-person wooden desk that I FELT IT. I felt the pressure building near my rectum. I began to pray. "Dear God, please don't let this happen. I'll do anything, just please don't let this happen, right now."

The only noise in the room was that of pencils scratching and paper rustling.

It was then that I sneezed.

I sneezed and I farted.

I snarted.

The popular blonde girl in the seat next to me looked over, mouth agape, and whispered, "Was that you!?" I shook my head vehemently. "No!" I stared at my paper in front of me, but you know how you can see with your ears when you are focusing your eyes in front of you? I saw, and heard, AND FELT, the snickers of the children around me. Whispers of "Kim farted" circled the room.

GOD HAD BETRAYED ME.

You might think that getting older would make farts less traumatic, but you'd be wrong.

I was in my late 20s and my coworker had invited me to go to yoga with her.

Up dog, down dog, cry like a baby, my body was somewhere between a tree pose and a pretzel when I FELT IT.

"Dear God, please don't let this happen. I'll do anything, just please don't let this happen, right now."

God and my body betrayed me. With Enya as my witness, that little fart made a great noise in that small studio room. The only difference is that my coworker and the other yogis had the good grace to forego snickering "Kim farted" across the room.

These were the stories that I told in front of a Toastmasters audience, not once, not twice, but three times. My vulnerability, embarrassment, and exaggeration won me first place in two speech contests and third place in another.

"Farts Help My Prayer Life" is not the best speech I've ever written. It is certainly not a speech on the most controversial, challenging, or inspirational of topics. But it was a pivotal moment for me. Why?

Because I was able to take these moments which had caused me so much emotional distress and share them. When I shared them, they became smaller. I had doctors and nurses and women who had older brothers turn to me and say, "Kim, farts are not a big deal. They are physical. They are a part of life."

Lesson #13: To be empowered and authentic, own your embarrassing moments.

I am authentically disgusted and embarrassed by farts. I used to feel ashamed of them. But now I have the courage to talk about them, laugh about them, and even give speeches in front of my peers about them. You have to have the courage to own your embarrassing moments in order to be authentic.

I think it is fitting that I mention courage in the same sentence as authenticity. But I want to take it a little deeper. What is authenticity? I have had a lot of time to think about this, ponder it, live it, try it, and revise it.

Authenticity is where confidence and humility intersect. Let me say that again. What is authenticity? It is where humility refines confidence, where confidence bolsters humility. You cannot have authenticity without both. You must be humble enough to remove the rose-colored glasses but also confident enough, strong enough, courageous enough to do so. To look at yourself with both humility and confidence. To enter relationships with both humility and confidence. To pursue your passions with both humility and confidence. My passion and purpose have to be bigger than my ego but I also have to have courage and confidence to live out the higher purpose for which I, and only I, was created.

What about the most embarrassing moments in your own life? Can you own them? Can you love them?

What would it mean for you to share them?

So, my dear fabulous divine traveler, how can you own your embarrassing moments?

~14~

Destroyer of Corporate Culture

2017

It was the worst day of my entire career. Honestly, it was almost like the beginning of a bad joke: the owner of the company, the COO (her husband), the VP Operations, the HR Manager, and my Manager walked into a bar.

Okay. Not a joke and not a bar. They called me into a board room for an unscheduled meeting. I just knew I was getting fired.

The owner's husband begins the meeting with "Kim, your negative attitude is destroying our corporate culture."

Holy shit.

Me? My negative attitude? Destroying corporate culture? Fuck!!!!

His words were a gut punch. I was in shock and embarrassed.

He continued. He had a yellow legal-size notepad in front of him. He had bullet points. He proceeded to list off all of my many transgressions – known and unknown – that I had committed over the past 15 months.

At one point I started to defend myself, speak up, try to explain, but I was cut off. This wasn't that kind of meeting.

So I started crying. For the next 45 minutes, tears streamed down my face in front of my colleagues and bosses while every one of my actions and motivations was discussed in detail.

The time that two members of upper management came to our campus to have a meeting with us and asked, "How did the summer go?" Each of us directors looked at each other and finally I spoke up. Addressed the elephant in the room. Told upper management what we had all been saying when they weren't around – that doing a renovation of our office and moving everything around without our input during the hardest and most busy time of the year was really difficult.

I thought it was courage. They interpreted my speaking up as negativity.

The time that I went to HR after one of my coworkers was accused of impropriety and stated that, based on my background in risk management, I thought that lack of systems within the company were creating risk and offered suggestions for what those changes in systems could be.

I thought it was prudent. They interpreted my speaking up as negativity.

For 15 months my bosses and managers had been building a case against me, and today was the day when they laid it all out in front of me. Emails I had sent and comments I had made were dissected, sometimes taken out of context, and used as ammunition.

They talked and I listened. They accused and I cried. I stayed silent until the end, when they asked me, "Do you still want to work here?" I said, "Yes" through my tears. The meeting ended and they left.

Later, the COO sent me an email saying something to the effect of, "I'm sorry we had to have that meeting but I'm glad you want to improve."

In this moment, I had a choice.

For just over two years I had been in Toastmasters and during that time, I learned the value of feedback. For five years I had been practicing gratitude. So good or bad, this was my response:

"I'm sorry for putting you in this position. I appreciate the feedback and opportunity to improve," and I MEANT IT.

Lesson #14: Take responsibility for your life.

It would have been so easy to continue to be a victim. I have been practicing victimhood my whole life. But I had made a choice not to be a victim anymore. I had made a choice to embrace appreciation IN EVERY CIRCUMSTANCE – not just the easy ones. I had made a choice to look at all feedback as an opportunity.

When I said that I was sorry I had put them in that position and that I appreciated the feedback, I meant it.

Do I wish that they had handled this situation differently? Yes! I wish that they had come to me sooner, corrected mistakes I was making before they became habits, made it a conversation, and asked me about my intentions instead of assigning them. I wish they had responded differently.

But I don't have any control over other people. I only have control over myself and my response to others.

I chose appreciation and empowerment.

I reached out to one of my mentors, Tim, and told him about the situation. Asked him for his advice.

He had experienced the situation so frequently he had a name for it. He called it the "Ugly Baby." Basically, he told me everybody thinks that babies are all beautiful and cute and wonderful, but in reality, there are some ugly babies. Parents will ask you, "Isn't my baby cute?" In that moment, what do you do? How do you respond when it's an ugly baby?

Well, most of us in this situation, would fib and say, "What a cute precious baby" and give the parents the affirmation they are looking for.

We know that the parents don't want honesty, they want affirmation. Out of love or kindness or friendship, we choose to give it to them.

When it comes to work, however, the answer doesn't seem as obvious. Tim was a media consultant. He was an expert in SEO and websites. Often, he would come in as a consultant to work with a small business owner. He learned early in his career that many a website was an "ugly baby." The owner had designed it herself and was emotionally invested in it. Another owner had taken some design classes and put hours of work into his site. These proud business owners would then ask Tim, "What do you think of my website?!"

When Tim would make suggestions or even propose a new launch, the owners became defensive. Even though they were literally paying him for his expertise and had even asked him what he thought, their emotional investment in their ugly babies precluded their receptivity to feedback.

Tim said that he learned that before giving his opinion he would ask, "Are you asking for affirmation or honesty?" or some variation of that question.

This was an important lesson for me to learn. This lesson has helped me in my relationships and in my career. Sometimes I just ask myself the question, "Is this person looking for affirmation or honesty?" before responding. I am extremely grateful for this lesson and for the meeting that taught it to me.

At this point I had also learned that humor is my superpower, as I described in Find The Funny. Instead of being sad and embarrassed about my negative attitude destroying corporate culture, I turned it around. I became "KIM STORY – DESTROYER OF

CORPORATE CULTURE." Who knew I was that important or powerful? I certainly hadn't! (Wouldn't Destroyer of Corporate Culture look GREAT on a coffee mug?!)

I laughed and I worked. I kept my mouth shut, projecting only positivity and affirmation in the workplace unless I knew someone was actually looking for critical feedback.

Two years later I was promoted. I was told that my leadership and people skills would be valuable at our newest location where we needed to improve morale and bring in clientele. I received my first official management role! Not too shabby for "The Destroyer of Corporate Culture"!

Six months after I was promoted, someone on my team was accused of having his "Negative attitude corrode the campus culture." I was heartbroken for him. I knew he had been giving feedback that he thought was helpful and important. His intentions had been misjudged. I knew the feeling.

I was so grateful that I had experienced it first. I could relate to what he was going through and as his leader, talk him through it.

I told him that I had been in a similar situation before, that it didn't last, and that I even ended up promoted.

I turned it into a joke, telling him that he was only a small fry, negatively impacting a campus. He had a lot of work to do before he caught up to Kim Story – Destroyer of Corporate Culture.

I earned his loyalty because I went to bat for him. I stood up for him. I listened to him. I related to him. I knew that his intentions had been good. But, unfortunately, he had spoken up about an ugly baby. I even had the opportunity to share the ugly baby story with him and pass on the lesson I had learned.

He accepted the lesson but also found a new job within the next three months. It made me sad that I had lost one of my favorite reports because of the accusations from someone who never tried to understand his intentions.

The lesson remains. All feedback is feedback. You get to choose how you respond to it. You can choose to be empowered or to be a victim. You can also choose to ignore the "ugly babies" in your life, condemning those who speak with honesty, OR you can actively solicit feedback to improve them.

Thank you, Toastmasters, for teaching me to take responsibility and always respond with, "I appreciate the feedback."

So, my dear fabulous divine traveler, how can you take more responsibility for your life?

RIP Tim Vasquez 9/20/60 – 3/27/23

I also appreciate his help and suggestions that made this book a possibility. I'm just sorry I didn't finish it in time for him to see it completed.

~15~

It's the Mentor I Became

2017 or 2018

About five or six years ago, I went with a couple of my friends to a YCP – Young Catholic Professionals event. The speaker that evening was Chris Tanco, COO of 7-Eleven. (Small company. You've probably never heard of it).

I was really excited to hear him speak. He talked about faith in the workplace and having a work-life balance. He listed off books he liked, such as *Good to Great* (I've read that). I waited throughout his whole talk, but he never addressed my burning question.

After he finished, I waited in line for 30 minutes or more to ask him my question: How did you find your mentors?

At this point I had been in Toastmasters for a few years and had learned the importance of finding good mentors. I was looking for mentors in my own life. I wanted direction. I wanted better. I had mentors in Toastmasters, but I wanted mentors in business, in my career. Where would I find them? Chris had to know.

I reached the front of the line. This was my moment. I was ready. I asked him, "Chris, I've heard about the importance of mentors and mentoring in business. How did you find yours?"

He cocked his head, looking thoughtful. He took a second before responding. His response was NOT what I was expecting.

He said, "It wasn't the mentors I found but the mentor I became that helped me get where I am."

He continued to tell me about his experience at Yum! Brands before he was hired at 7-Eleven. He was on a team and would work with his people. One of them got promoted. Then another. Then another. Enough people received promotions that it drew the attention of his superiors. They started asking, "What is going on with that group?"

Their answers led them to Chris.

It was his investment in others' success that has led him to his own continued career success.

Zig Ziglar wouldn't be surprised at all by this. In fact, the next lesson is a direct quote from Zig.

Lesson #15: You can have anything you want in life if you just help enough other people get what they want.

This lesson is true for sales, education, marriage, family, and friendships.

I knew my husband wanted to get married again after his divorce and wanted to have a family. It happened.

As a salesperson, communicator, trainer, and presenter, I am always thinking about the "WIIFM" (what's in it for me) for the people with whom I interact. It's not about ME making a sale, it's about YOU receiving a product that is a solution to a problem. It's not about ME standing on stage, it's about YOU and your need for personal development and answers.

A few years ago, I was elected to be a Division Director in Toastmasters. I would be mentoring five Area Directors who would each be mentoring and supporting four-to-six Toastmasters clubs.

At one point I angered one of my Area Directors. Bindu had come to me with a question, expecting that, as her leader, I would provide the answer. Instead I responded with, "What do you think you should do?" I answered her question with a question and that was NOT what she was looking for.

We have since joked about this experience on her *Inspire and Empower* podcast and she has even told this story on stage during a keynote speech. I was not a leader who told people what to do. I was a leader who mentored and developed the people around me into better versions of themselves. By asking Bindu to think of a solution for herself, I helped her to grow.

Since then, she has also served as a Division Director in Toastmasters. She has been a TED Talk presenter and received a John Maxwell certification. Bindu is paying it forward, becoming a leader through mentoring.

I mentioned in Destroyer of Corporate Culture that I had been promoted into a management role. I am still in contact with some of my mentees from that time. I've been told I was "the best boss" one woman had ever had. In my role I worked with teenagers as well as adults. I had the opportunity to help one teen find confidence by allowing him to expand his role and get promoted. By the time he left for college, he could do many of the tasks that my adult peers were performing.

True leaders are talent scouts. Mentorship is finding out about the desires, goals, and dreams of the people around you, believing in them, and equipping them with the tools to help get what they want. This is necessary for you in turn to be able to get what you want.

So, my dear fabulous divine traveler, who could you help get what they want?

~16~

I'm Fat, I'm Ugly, and I Have No Friends

1997

It was a Saturday night and I was so excited to go to the monthly dance for teens that was offered at the other middle school in our town. I was in seventh grade and ridiculously nerdy and awkward, but I loved music and dancing. I had taken ballet, jazz, and gymnastics classes and just loved the feeling of moving my body to the music.

I also liked the fact that I had friends who were going to be there at the dance. The great thing about having skipped third grade meant that I was a year younger than my classmates. What this meant was that the girls who were on my recreational soccer team were all a grade below me, since our team assignments were based on age. They all thought I was really cool! I was a grade above them and a decent soccer player. With them, I was in my element.

Which was such a nice reprieve from the bullying that took place with the kids in my own grade. To them, I was NOT cool.

There were a lot of mean things that were said about me, to my face, and behind my back. I never felt like I fit in, and if I made a friend at school, I always wondered when they were going to let everyone else talk them out of it.

I was really looking forward to the dance.

I arrived, found my friends in the cafeteria, chatted, and then headed back to the gymnasium to listen to the music.

As I was walking in, a boy from my class started walking toward me. I thought to myself, "Is this the moment? Is he going to ask me to dance?" I waited with nervous excitement as he did, in fact, approach me and said, "Kim, I have a question for you."

"Oh?"

"Do you wax your forehead?"

"What? Excuse me?"

"Do you wax your forehead?" he repeated then burst out laughing, looking back at the bleachers and the crowd of guys who erupted in hysterics behind him.

I stared down at my feet, mumbled something that resembled the word "No," turned on my heel and headed briskly out of the gymnasium toward the bathroom. I was honestly too shocked to cry. (Don't worry, that came later.)

I am well aware of the fact that I have a ginormous, shiny forehead. When I was born, I was also bald – so bald that my mom had to tape bows to my head to make sure people knew I was a girl. My dad said that as an infant I looked like a football attached to a body.

What can I say? I needed an extra-large head to fit all my brains. Unfortunately, brains were not particularly attractive to the seventh-grade guys at the dance that night.

I was a depressed, socially awkward kid. I often thought to myself, "If I died, no one would care." In eighth grade, I was a little bit of a cutter and still have the scars from where I self-tattooed my name on my wrist with a push pin. I was screwed up enough that cutting myself made me feel better. It made me feel better to feel on the outside the way I was feeling on the inside. Pain was my friend. Physical pain was a release.

My negative self-talk did not improve with the hormones of my teenage years. In fact, I have always had physically and emotionally destructive periods, where I get intensely depressed for the 24 hours before "Aunt Flow" officially comes to visit. Every time I would find myself repeating and feeling, "I'm fat, I'm ugly, and I have no friends."

It didn't matter years later when I went to college that I was 112 lbs of pure muscle. It didn't matter how many guys told me I was beautiful or attractive. It didn't matter how many people I had in my life who loved me and enjoyed my company. It was never enough.

So, what's changed?

Lesson #16: Eliminate negative self-talk. You are beautiful and you are loved.

This is a chapter that I almost didn't include. But during one of the revisions of this book I realized I would be remiss if I talked to women about Empowerment and never addressed the topic of self-image.

I don't feel like I am an expert on this topic. I don't actually think I'm particularly attractive. As I'm writing this, I am 5'1", 200 lbs, and a size 14. I've gained weight and lost weight many times in my life and have felt the effects on my esteem when it happens. It's a challenge. I like pizza more than I like diets.

I think that my hair is too thin and I don't like my eyebrows. I always wanted to be 5'3" (like the *Baby Got Back* song!) My skin is starting to show signs of age. I wish I turned tan in the summer instead of red. In the winter my legs just look purple and blotchy in the cold.

But when I watched the Barbie movie a couple months ago, I realized I had to say something. I had to say something about the impossible demands we put on ourselves and how much we link our worth with our looks.

I had to say something about the unending criticism that I've had to confront in my own life. (Mostly from myself.) I had to say something about the effects of hormones on my self-talk and how challenging it has been to love myself.

I want you to know that you are so beautiful. That you are so loved. That you can eliminate that negative self-talk from your life. No matter what has been said to you in the past, no matter what your actual physical appearance, none of it fucking matters.

I am fucking beautiful. I am deeply loved. You, my precious reader, are beautiful and loved beyond compare, and I wish I could (lovingly) shout it at you. Your essence is precious and eternal. No one can take that away from you…except you.

So don't.

I have started writing in my gratitude journal, "I'm so thankful for my beauty. I'm so thankful for my body. I'm so grateful I am so loved, that I have so much love in my life." If I can do it, you can too.

So, my dear fabulous divine traveler, do you know how beautiful and loved you are?

~17~

But I'll Be Homeless

2015–2017

After breaking off my engagement to FF, my dad and I moved into an apartment together. He couldn't afford to live by himself and even I had only recently received a job that made living on my own possible. It made sense for us to help each other out financially by splitting bills and sharing an apartment.

It didn't take long before it became a toxic situation. I continued to choose to love my dad, but he wasn't always a great guy. I was already paying more than half the rent because he couldn't afford more. He found money for alcohol though.

He didn't have a driver's license or car, but he did have cirrhosis. None of that stopped him from having me drive him for his weekly liquor store stock up.

We lived in an active apartment community. We made friends and played water volleyball and cooked out on the weekends. It was fun, but Dad being my roommate and in my friend group was awkward and unhealthy. He was unafraid to talk about me when I wasn't around, and I didn't love some of the things that would get back to me. He could also be an angry drunk and I found his behavior embarrassing.

I listened from my bedroom as he poured drinks at all hours of the day and night. I listened as he killed himself one ice cube at a time. Clink, clink, clink, pour. One vodka tonic at a time.

He was also gambling – a lot. He had notebooks and notepads of bets he had made. Phone calls to God-knows-who at all hours of the day and night. He came to watch one of my speech contests but had to excuse himself to the hallway where he proceeded to yell at someone over the phone about some bet he had made.

He kept telling me just how much money he was making and pressured me to "invest" like he was. He even tried to coerce a guy I was dating to give him money because "It was guaranteed profits." (Then why was he so broke?)

I was unhappy. I was tired of Dad making his problems my responsibility.

One night I went to watch the movie, *The Shack*, with my friend Jen. It's one of my favorite books and the lessons about who God really is, about free will and judgment, why bad things happen to good people, and what God's unconditional love looks like have been instrumental in my own healing. It was a powerful reminder, especially given the living situation with my dad. I cried and cried and cried. The main character in the movie struggles with his relationship with his abusive father and what it means to forgive. It struck a chord with me.

Jen has been one of my closest friends since we met during our freshman year in college. I love her because she is practical, hard-working, ambitious, caring, and a woman of faith, but most importantly, she values love. She has been learning and practicing leadership skills since long before I even knew that was a thing. She is also incredibly skilled at setting boundaries.

Jen and I went to Applebees after the movie. As we talked over appetizers and $3 Long Islands, I started crying again. I was unhappy but I felt responsible for my dad. To Jen, the answer was clear: I had to move out. I needed a physical boundary between myself and my father's demands.

I agreed with her and started doing the math. Our lease was up in four months. If I signed the shortest lease then that could maybe only be 11 months. That would be long enough for Dad to find a new place to live.

Jen listened as I talked, then she said, "Kim, you have four months left on your lease. If four months isn't long enough for your dad to figure it out, 11 months won't change anything for him. It will needlessly extend your misery."

Her words hit me and a million objections came rising up my throat. A million excuses that had become a habit. I opened my mouth to spout some of my codependent programming, but Jen just looked at me and the words died on my lips.

I said, "You're right."

That week was awful. Every day, knowing I had to tell Dad I was moving out, every day, dreading the conversation.

Finally, I ripped off the Band-Aid and told him. He took it about the way I expected. Angry, he shouted at me, "It's your fault I'll be homeless. It's your fault I'll end up under a bridge!"

Those words hurt. His anger hurt. But I stayed calm and stood my ground. I said that we had four months to try and find him a roommate.

He stormed off to the bar and proceeded to tell everyone who would listen what a horrible daughter I was. I know because I started to get phone calls asking me, "How can you do this to your dad?"

The next four months weren't great. Dad found someone who needed a place to live and moved him into our living room while I was still there. Once I had a new place, Dad moved this guy into my bedroom before I had finished moving my stuff out of the room. Dad lied to me about how much money this guy was giving him and coerced me into paying more than my share of rent. Remember how I said in I'm Just Lucky To Be Alive that sometimes life puts The Squeeze on us and in those moments we give back what we've been absorbing? Well, my dad had been absorbing alcoholic, drunk, angry resentments and The Squeeze that was put on him directed all that negativity my way. It was not my favorite time.

But I was happy and I was relieved. There was a light at the end of the tunnel.

Lesson #17: Develop healthy boundaries.

I am so grateful that I have a friend like Jen who could see what I couldn't: I was not responsible for my father. She knew that if I didn't establish boundaries with him now, it wouldn't ever happen, and it would destroy my life. She loved me enough to tell me I deserved better.

Even today as I type this, I find it difficult. Difficult to say that I walked away from my dad. I think as women, we are programmed to be caregivers. Growing up with a codependent mom and a dad who never respected boundaries, I never learned to set them.

My physical and emotional boundaries were violated over and over as I grew up as a child. I would tell Dad that he was hurting me when he grabbed my arm and he would say, "You need to toughen up." I would say that my feelings had been hurt and he would also say, "You need to toughen up." I learned that when people hurt me that I needed to accept it. Their actions were my responsibility. Dad's ego and feelings were also my responsibility. There is data that shows children of alcoholics are extremely empathetic. It's a survival skill, navigating the emotional minefield that is an alcoholic home. This is very true in my life. I have to be careful because I still feel other people's feelings as strongly as my own and even have difficulty in determining how I feel, difficulty separating my feelings from those of the people around me.

During my teen years, Mom would overshare about her relationship with my dad and use me as her counselor and confidant. I would find nasty notes that they wrote to each other about everything from finances to sex.

As I got older, I craved affection. I craved love and security. Like so many women, I tried to find it in sexuality and attention from the opposite sex. I was promiscuous. I was afraid to say no to men once I had their attention. I'm not proud to say it, but I couldn't really be raped because I never said no. I was a willing victim of my own codependence.

I tell you all of this to show you how awful I was at boundaries. I tell you all of this to show you that setting boundaries is a skill – and a vital, essential one at that – and you can learn it!

I highly recommend the book *Boundaries* by Dr. Cloud and Dr. Townsend. It was a game changer for me and helped me to stay strong during those times when I have wanted to cave in to the wants, needs, and demands of others.

A couple years after I moved out from my dad, I was living alone in my own apartment. I had been dating a guy for about a year, we will call him "Drummer Boy", and I thought we were in love. We decided that he would move in with me.

Drummer Boy had already put in his notice at his complex but still had about a month before we were to move in together. Something in my gut said it was a bad idea. That it wasn't right. The timing wasn't right and that I would regret it.

So I sat him down and said I was sorry. I still wanted to be with him, but I wasn't ready for us to live together yet.

I'll never forget his response, "But I'll be homeless!"

Déjà vu much?!

Thankfully, I had experience with this already. I responded, "You are a 41-year-old man who has a job. You are not going to be homeless."

He broke up with me.

I was sad and I missed him, but I knew I had made the right decision. I trusted my intuition. It was not time for us to move in together. Ultimately, as it turned out, he was not the right guy for me.

Learning and practicing boundaries has increased my confidence. I have boundaries on my time, boundaries on my body, and boundaries on my emotions. I also have boundaries on how I allow others to treat me. I am not afraid to walk away, physically or emotionally, when I am not being treated well.

Boundaries are how you respect yourself. When you respect yourself, you increase your confidence. When you have confidence and respect for yourself, life is happier and better.

I encourage you to find a "boundaries mentor." Someone you can trust, trust their judgment, and who you can see practices boundaries in her life.

Additionally, one exercise I find helpful is, when you are facing a difficult decision and wonder what to do, think about a woman you love. Your mother, daughter, or best friend. Think about someone you love and want the best for.

What advice would you give her in this situation?

I have found that we will tolerate a lot more crap in our lives and mistreatment from others than we will ever tolerate for the people we love. Why are we so courageous in our love for others and leave none of it for ourselves?

So, my dear fabulous divine traveler, what boundaries do you need to put in place?

~18~

Football, Claws, and a Black Eye

2001

It was Christmas Break after my first semester of college. I was excited to see my hometown friends who I had missed for the last six months.

"Kim! It's so great to see you! Wait! What? Do you STILL have a black eye?!"

"Um, well, no...this is a new one," I sheepishly replied.

Of course, they wanted to know the story. The last time they had seen me, at summer camp, I had gotten a black eye playing ultimate frisbee. (I know, who the hell gets a black eye playing ultimate frisbee? This girl, apparently.)

In fact, there were pictures of me from senior night at camp – the night that everyone dressed up in their prom dresses and suits one last time – with full makeup, hair, prom dress and heels...and a blackeye.

So what HAD happened now?

95

I was an athletic chick when I left for college and I loved sports. I met another Kim who also lived on the fourth floor of my dorm. She had an older brother who loved to play flag football. Kim and I and our friends would get together from time to time throughout the semester to play and it was a blast.

As our first semester in college drew to a close, we learned about "Reading Days." Days when you didn't have class because you were supposed to be studying for finals.

BWAHAHAHAHA.

Reading Days were awesome! College without classes? The best!

We scheduled another flag football evening. Kim's suitemate Jen came out. It was a coed game and two of the guys were captains. They chose the other guys first. Sexist is as sexist does, lol. When it was only girls left, Jen and I were chosen first, for opposing teams.

Jen was also extremely athletic. Strong and competitive. It was natural that we would be marking up on each other.

Her team had the ball, they threw it to Jen. I ran after her. If I sorta kinda ended up clawing her neck as I tried to BRING HER DOWN…oops!

Play continued. A light rain began. The game was tied and it was fourth down for the other team. This would be the final play to determine the victors before we would have to call it.

I marked up tight on Jen. There was no way in hell that she was getting the ball when so much was at stake.

She ran away from me, she tried to shrug me off, but I was on her. She used her elbows to create space. (Something she still does when we go to concerts together. Very effective!)

Elbows out, calling for the ball, pushing and jostling, she tried harder as I marked her closer.

She swung her arm out, elbow first, intending to push me away, but

THUNK!

Her elbow connected with that place where my forehead met my nose. I crumpled. She shouted to her teammates, "I'm open! I'm open!" To her incredible chagrin, they came to check on me instead, the game forgotten.

As the rain increased, they pulled me to my feet and the game was over.

Jen and I have told that story many times over the last two decades. How she gave me a blackeye, but I clawed her neck. How she found mud in her ears for days after that game because of my voracity. (Still hilarious.)

Jen and I have been a match for each other in so many more ways than just flag football. While we were in college, we lived in the same dorm building, went to the same church, and even got involved in the same youth outreach programs.

It turns out we were both from DFW and at the end of our freshman year in college, she gave me a ride home. We packed up her car with EVERY SINGLE POSSESSION, filling it to the brim, praying for 3½ hours as we drove from College Station to Carrollton that there wouldn't be any need for her to use the rearview mirror.

We stayed in touch when I went to grad school in North Carolina and when she did Teach For America in LA. We stayed in touch when she lived in Poland for five years while pursuing a degree in dentistry.

When she moved back and we were both looking to meet more young adults who shared our faith, we started a young adults ministry at her church together.

When I was looking for answers as to why I had screwed up my life so badly, she came to the book club I started.

Later, after joining Toastmasters, I found out she had been a member of Toastmasters years before. She joined again at my behest.

When I wanted to start a Toastmasters club in my hometown, she was a charter member. When she had to give "The Roast" as a project for speech credit, I was her chosen victim. In front of my peers, she embarrassed me, regaling them with stories of my competitive nature, not just the scars from our flag football scuffle but also her roommates' fear after playing Candyland with someone of my nature and the number of expletives I used on what should have been a "friendly game night."

When she became a Division Director in Toastmasters and someone was no longer able to fill the role of Area Director on her team, she asked me to step up, and I did.

Jen and I have traveled together, gone to concerts and museums together, cried together, laughed together, and served our communities together. She was a bridesmaid in my wedding.

She is the same Jen from the last chapter, But I'll Be Homeless. She is the one who has told me hard truths when I needed to hear them. She is the one who saw potential in me when I didn't see it in myself. I am inspired by her and look up to her and respect her, but she also respects me and my opinions and advice. It is a mutual friendship.

Lesson #18: When someone who loves you speaks truth – listen and act.

One of my biggest frustrations in being friends with other women is when I know that I am providing great advice, in a spirit of love, and a woman nods her head in agreement, saying "Yeah, you're right," and then...does nothing.

I had one friend who said that, "Whenever someone gives me advice, even though I know it's right, I just feel compelled to do the opposite."

I don't understand. I don't get it. Why?

Is it that we think we don't deserve happiness? Is it that we care more about other people than we do ourselves? Is it that we don't know who to listen to? Is it that we only listen to the critics?

A few years back, I heard some advice that I'm going to share with you. "Don't accept criticism from someone you wouldn't go to for advice." Haters and trolls on social media? Fuck 'em. They don't matter. Unless it is someone that you would go to for advice, don't accept their criticism.

I was at a networking luncheon about ten years ago when one of the leaders said, "Well, dogs don't bark at parked cars." Huh? I didn't understand so I asked him to explain. He said, "Think about it; dogs don't bark at parked cars. They only bark at moving ones. So it is with criticism. The only way to keep from being criticized is not to be doing anything. But once you start moving, you WILL receive criticism. So what? Keep moving anyway."

If you're doing anything in life, you're going to get criticized. So what? Don't listen to someone's criticism unless you would also listen to their advice.

Well, Kim, how do I know who to go to for advice?

I'm so glad you asked. Only get advice from someone who has what you want. If she is in a shitty relationship, why do you keep asking her for advice about your own? If she has shitty health habits, why would you try to emulate her? If she's unappreciated in a dead-end job or her kids don't treat her with respect, why do you keep thinking she will magically have the answers to help you be respected and appreciated?

Now that I've shared all this, what does it have to do with the rest of this chapter?

I gave the whole history of my relationship with Jen to show you a few things. First, I knew she loved me and knew me. She has only ever wanted the best for me. She has invested in her own personal development so that she continues to learn and grow and be a better person.

This means that she meets the prerequisites for the above-mentioned caveats. She has developed strong boundaries in her own life and has done well for herself in her own career. She is someone from whom I would go to for advice AND will even listen to her criticisms.

All those years ago, sitting across from each other at Applebee's, I KNEW she was speaking TRUTH to me, out of LOVE. That is what it means to have a best friend. She was confident enough in herself and in our relationship to tell me something I didn't want to hear.

But what came next was all on me. I ACTED on what she said. I didn't let it go in one ear and out the other. I didn't just agree with her to her face and then continue to allow myself to suffer needlessly. I didn't spend the next few months complaining about my dad and my living situation, without working toward the solution.

Even though it was hard, I took action.

My friendship with Jen has made me a better person. Ladies, we are stronger together.

If we want empowerment, then we also need connection. We need other women in our lives who support us, love us, and empower us. We need people in our lives with whom we can share our feelings without shame or guilt. We need a safe place to be able to share our ugly so that it doesn't consume us. We need women who speak truth to us, out of love.

One of the first things that abusers do is try to cut women off from their friends and family. They make us feel alone. And then, when we are alone, they smother us with shame. That is how we can be controlled. That is how invisible prisons are created. Prisons that destroy our power.

We need to have people with whom we can be our authentic selves. With whom we can share the good and the bad. Laugh and cry together. Mutual friendships where we are able to both give and receive. Where there is trust.

The Law of Attraction says that "what you want wants you." If you are still looking for friends like this, trust me, there are women out there who are looking for a friend just like you. Who need you and your gifts. Who need your insight and support. Who need your perspective, your truths, and your support to follow through with action.

Women with strong social ties are harder to "break." Women who have encouragers in their corner are harder to shame. Women who have other women saying, "Know your worth" are less likely to forget it.

Can we all be those kinds of women? Can we create these strong bonds? Can we build up our communities? Can we build up each other? Do we have the strength to speak truth out of love? Do we have the courage to act when those we love tell us hard truths?

I believe we can. I know we can.

So, my dear fabulous divine traveler, can you act when you hear hard truths spoken in love?

~19~

I Am Inevitable (an unlikely love story)

2015–2019

"We are never getting together. I don't love you."

The date was July 4, 2019, and Chris and I had had yet ANOTHER conversation about how he just didn't believe that we were ever going to be a couple.

Chris and I had dated off and on since his divorce and my canceled engagement four years prior. We had become friends because of the shared heartbreak of our situations and bonded and consoled each other during those difficult times. I know you're wondering, so, yes, we did "console" each other. Hey, a girl has needs. Also, the sex with Chris was the best I ever had in my whole life and I didn't really want to stop having it.

There was just this pesky problem of him not feeling the same way I felt about him.

You see, over the past four years I had fallen in love with Chris. I loved his sense of humor, his loyalty to his friends and family, and his patient and easy-going nature. He was so very

103

different from so many of the men I had dated. He was kind and very, very slow to anger. He didn't yell or criticize or condemn. We had many interests in common. We loved being in the swimming pool and throwing pool parties or playing water volleyball. We loved sci fi and fantasy (him a little more sci fi and me a little more fantasy). We loved board games and game nights. It was Chris who introduced me to Minute to Win It and Jackbox. He was even in an all-Asian (except him) board game group, his pale whiteness towering above his darker-skinned, but shorter, counterparts in group photos.

Mostly I just loved how I felt when I was with him. It was easy and comfortable. Even he would laud the comfort level during the time we spent together. We were both, just, OURSELVES.

I loved the way that I would ask if I could come over and his predictable response, "Of course."

But he still protested that "Us" was never going to happen.

I tried to date other guys. I did online dating and met someone who was, all right. I got set up with another guy (Drummer Boy from But I'll Be Homeless) by a friend in Toastmasters, and Drummer Boy and I dated for over a year. We even discussed moving in together. Drummer Boy had even given notice at his apartment complex. But when it finally came time to pull the trigger and move him in, I couldn't do it. I missed Chris.

Still, I knew it was never going to happen with Chris. I also knew I would probably never find another guy like Chris. So sometime around 4th of July when Chris looked me deeply and honestly in the eyes, declaring it would never happen, I agreed. I told him I wanted to spend time with him anyway.

I loved him even when he didn't love me back. I wanted to be around him and do things with him even when the emotional security of a relationship was off the table.

That following September, we were with a group of friends when I was introduced to someone I hadn't met before. Her name was Sara, and Sara had just randomly started crying. Being an empathetic person, I asked what was going on. She proceeded to tell me that her second husband had just told her he was leaving her and she thought she was going to be getting divorced, again.

Sara and Chris had known each other since middle school and after consoling her and befriending her, I let her know that she should also talk to Chris. That he had been my friend after my engagement ended and was really level-headed and supportive. She was incredibly grateful and the three of us spent a lot of time together that day.

The next time I saw her, she told me that the divorce was in fact going to happen and that, after the initial shock, it was probably a blessing in disguise. She said, "Kim, I want to travel! My ex-husband didn't want to travel and I have miles I need to use. I'm going to take a vacation to Mexico, do you want to come with me?" Of course I energetically responded, "Yes, totally," even though I believed in my heart that a vacation with this girl that I had only met twice would never actually come to fruition.

I could not have been more wrong.

Within days she started sending me flight info and talking dates. I didn't know then, but I know now, that Sara is an AMAZING PLANNER and EXCELLENT in follow-thru. I am extremely lucky to count her as one of my best friends and travel buddies.

It's funny because I remember having an internal conversation with myself that went something like this, "Kim, every year for a New Year's resolution you say you want to travel. Now, you have someone who is planning out the entire trip and all you have to do is pay your part and show up? And you would be adding to the happiness of a broken-hearted woman just by being there? What's your excuse for not going?"

Yes, I talk to myself. Frequently in fact.

I couldn't think of a good reason not to go, so I said yes and started to book my ticket. I decided to ask if Sara would mind if Chris came, since she had known him for so long and I just really enjoyed his company. She said the more the merrier and that is how the three of us ended up on a plane to Mexico City in November of 2019.

We stayed with one of Sara's friends, an archaeologist turned Episcopal priest who had met his wife on a dig site (I know! How cool is that?!) Fr. Matthew asked us if we wanted a tour of Mexico City and the history of the Aztec site of Tenochtitlan. (Um, YES!)

After some very yummy tacos al pastor from a small storefront, we proceeded to spend the morning on our own personal guided tour of the remains of Tenochtitlan. It was amazing! The biggest shock of all came when we were inside the museum and Chris' look of astonishment and awe as he learned about "face knives." It was so silly and gleeful and something happened in my heart. What is a face knife? Think of your typical hand-carved stone knife but then take chiclets for teeth and add googly eyes. Now think of an enemy Aztec conducting their ritual sacrifice and the last thing that happens to you, as their captive, is one of the googly-eyed, chiclet-grinning knives slicing open your chest to remove your heart. It's sadistically humorous!

Something opened up in Chris during that trip. Some of the tenseness and reserve that he had been carrying with him since his own divorce seemed to melt away. The next day the five of us (Sara, Chris, Matthew, his wife Heather, and I) traveled to Xochimilco to experience the river boats. If you have not done the Xochimilco canal cruise, even I will be hard put to describe it in words. The boats are colorful and vibrant. The atmosphere is energetic and a little frenetic. There is the sound of mariachi in the air occasionally interrupted by the jostling – and bumping – of boats along the crowded water corridor. What would be street vendors in a town are now tiny canoes full of their wares darting in and out of the larger and slower boat traffic. We indulged in drinks served in coconuts and elotes smeared with butter, mayo, cotija, and spices. We hailed and were hailed by boats overloaded with five generations of a local familia or other gringos enjoying the fun and the chaos, so different from that of our homeland. We all laughed and smiled and took videos and just enjoyed ourselves, Chris included.

There were other highlights from that trip, but they don't bear importance to the story of what came next.

Chris and I were on the plane next to each other headed back to DFW. We were reminiscing about all of the great times we had during our trip and just how seamlessly it had all fallen together. Actually, I guess there was one final highlight, the night before we headed back to the states, the five of us ended up having an impromptu pajama dance party with Matthew and Chris taking turns as our 70s, 80s, and 90s hits DJs. The next day on the plane, Chris and I were still laughing and on our "vacation high" talking about what a fantastic trip it had been.

At one point I said that I knew it wouldn't work with my exes because of the fights we had when traveling. For whatever reason, travel brings out stress, and in those already stressful relationships, I found that I didn't travel well with those men. I asked Chris whether he and his ex-wife had traveled well together.

He actually responded, "Yes." He paused for a moment, thinking, then continued. "With my ex-wife and me, travel was never the issue. In fact, I'll be honest. We had marriage problems just like a lot of people do. A lot of the problems in our marriage were my fault. It's just that I thought I had time to fix them. That we would be together and I had time. I was wrong. While many of the problems in our marriage were my fault, it was 100% her choice to leave and divorce. When it got tough, she left. I think differently about marriage than that."

Now it was my turn to take a second and ponder what he had just said. Then I got a knowing sparkle in my eye as I queried, "So you're saying you need someone a little more…stubborn…and persistent?"

Hesitantly he responded, "Yeah."

I immediately piped up saying, "Well, I happen to know someone like that."

He looked at me with something of a smirk, but also a hint of resignation and happy foreboding. "Yes, I think I do too."

~~Then he looked deeply in my eyes and told me he desperately loved me and wanted to be with me.~~

Nope. This isn't that kind of love story.

We got off the plane, said our goodbyes, and a few days later I went on a date with another guy. We will call this guy Racecar.

Racecar had asked me out before I went to Mexico. This would be our first date. (Remember, Chris had told me it was NEVER GOING TO HAPPEN BETWEEN US.)

Racecar took me out to dinner and we talked and had a good time. We talked about traveling and he said that if all went well, maybe we would end up traveling together. I had told Racecar that I was seeing someone else and later on during the date, Racecar started to ask questions about this other guy. I told him the truth, that I had feelings but that Chris and I had dated off and on for four years and he had said it was never going to happen.

Racecar then proceeded to tell me that he understood men and that IT WAS NEVER GOING TO HAPPEN WITH CHRIS AND ME. (At least everyone is giving consistent messaging.)

Racecar dropped me off and I told him that before anything else could happen between us, I would have to break things off with Chris.

Well....

Over the next couple days, Racecar started blowing up my phone. Even if what happened next with Chris had not occurred, I had already decided that Racecar was not the right guy for me.

I was standing next to my car, pumping gas (callback to I'm Lucky To Be Alive, I was making sure my tank was filled up!), when Chris called. He asked me if I wanted to participate in his family's Secret Santa Christmas Gift exchange that year.

Did I want to participate?

DID I WANT TO PARTICIPATE?!

I covered the phone, jumped up and down, maybe screamed a bit, and did my best Amy Santiago dance next to my car, then very calmly responded, "Why yes, sure, that sounds good." Talk about the understatement of the century!

I spent the next couple of days in limbo. Excited but not wanting to assume. Finally, Wednesday evening, the night before Thanksgiving in November 2019, I was sitting next to Chris on the edge of the bed and just couldn't hold back any longer.

"So, you invited me to your family's Secret Santa. I think that's a big deal, but I don't want to assume anything or read too much into anything. Chris, are we together?"

Chris responded, "Of course." (It was only then that I knew that every time he had said "of course" what he really meant was "I love you.")

Ecstatic and in shock, I caressed his hand in both of mine, looked deeply into his eyes, mustered up my best Thanos voice and said, "I am inevitable."

Who has two thumbs and is the queen of romance? This girl!

Lesson #19: True love is proactive, not reactive.

This is not the love story I dreamed of. It's not the Prince-Charming-overcoming-dragons-and-sea-witches and glass-slippers-to-be-reunited-with-his-one-true-love love story that I had always dreamed of.

True love looks nothing like what I imagined.

Whitney Houston's "How Will I Know?" rings in my ears as I type these words. The truth is, I didn't. I didn't know. In fact, I knew that it would never happen. I knew that he didn't love me.

But I loved him anyway.

My biggest mistake in dating, all my life, due to low self-esteem and misunderstandings about what it meant for a man to pursue a woman, was that my relationships were all reactive.

If a guy liked me, then that was enough. It didn't matter what I thought of him. If he liked me, I felt obligated to give him a chance. I also "dated down." I thought that if I dated a guy that I knew was unworthy of me, then he would treat me better. I was…mistaken.

Which is why I share my love story with you. We all know that Disney princess stories are bullshit. We know that they only show the beginning and that "Happily Ever After" doesn't even begin to encapsulate the actual day-to-day grind of marriage and loving someone long-term. (Don't get me wrong, I LOVE Disney princess movies and if you can sing all the words to "I Can Show You The World," you are my people.)

Disney gives us the sprint, but marriage is a marathon. Runners know that the two races require different muscle groups and stamina, and so it is with lasting relationships.

The problem for me is that I didn't have good examples to draw from. I didn't know what a good relationship looked like. I relied on my feelings. I was reactive.

Except with Chris.

I am grateful for the opportunity to have loved Chris for so long and so deeply before we ever got together. Marriage is tough. Being a stepmom is tough. Chris is THE ONLY MAN who is worth it. For anyone less, I'd be back in my single-bedroom, two-story townhome. Just me and my cat.

Chris is the only man for whom my love is proactive. Who I love even when it's difficult – especially when it's difficult. I love him enough to go to see my own personal therapist when my mental health starts to take a toll on our relationship. I love him enough to see a couple's therapist together, to head off problems and conflict before it happens.

I love him enough to bite my tongue when I want to say something mean. I love him enough to say "I'm sorry" when I am mean.

I've also learned to love others better. I've learned that all love is proactive. It's not reactive. It's not about what I get. It's not about the compliments and reciprocity and boosts to my self-esteem. The moments in which I am most loving toward others in my life is when I choose to give of myself and my gifts, without any expectation of anything in return. Often it's tough. Loving my stepson and loving him without expecting anything in return, is tough. I fail at it often. That doesn't mean that the principle, the lesson, is any less true.

Sometimes, it's a love story that's even better than what I could have ever imagined.

I remember the first time that, practicing gratitude and in awe of our being a couple, I looked at Chris and said, "I'm so lucky."

This man. This amazing, wonderful, kind, funny man of mine, who I never expected to be with, said to me, "No Kim. *We're* so lucky."

So, my dear fabulous divine traveler, how can your love be more proactive?

~20~

The Great Derailer

November 7, 2020

My husband and I got engaged on Thursday October 22, 2020. I was ecstatic. It had FINALLY happened. He proposed during a game night Zoom call with our friends, from our living room, which wasn't exactly the proposal of my dreams (I'm still waiting for the hot air balloon ride proposal I've dreamed of since I was in my early 20s), but it was the fall of 2020 and many of humanity's shared dreams and wishes were no longer coming to fruition. I focused on the elation of spending the rest of my life with the man I loved more than any other and less on the disappointments of circumstance.

I texted EVERYONE and posted to Facebook and reveled in the moment. I texted Dad "I said YES!" along with a picture of the ring.

No response.

A couple days later I sent a follow up text saying, "Hey, did you see my message?! Chris and I are engaged!" He texted back a quick "I saw the ring. Very pretty." Those would be the last words I ever heard from my father.

I texted him a couple more times over the next week. No response. This was actually typical and something my mother and I had worriedly discussed with my father, but to no avail. Finally, on Friday November 6, I started to get that feeling in my stomach that something just wasn't quite right. That I would need to check on him. I looked at my fiancé and said, if I haven't heard anything from my dad by tomorrow, I'm going to drive to check on him. Chris told me that he would come with me. It was our week with my soon-to-be stepson, so I was adamant that it was probably no big deal and that my fiancé should stay with his son. He refused (apparently I'm not the only one who can be stubborn and persistent).

I started texting a few of the people I knew from the apartment complex Dad lived in to see if anyone had seen him recently. No one responded that night and my uneasiness grew.

The next day, Chris' sister agreed to watch her nephew for us, and Chris and I proceeded to make the 45-minute drive to where my dad resided. I started to get responses to my inquiries. All of them were some variation of, "No, I haven't seen Cliff in a few weeks." At this point I was uneasy, mostly afraid that my father had fallen and couldn't get up and was lying in pain, but I still thought he was probably okay.

We parallel parked the car, entered the gate, walked up a flight of stairs to the second floor, and proceeded down the hallway to his apartment.

I knew it was his apartment because of the grocery bag of Meals on Wheels food delivery hanging on the outside doorknob. It was at that moment that my heart dropped and my stomach clenched. I walked the final paces to his door and looked in the bag. I touched what should have been a frozen dinner. It wasn't just room temperature, it was warm. At that moment, I knew. I knew, but I held on to that small shred of hope anyway.

I knocked.

No answer.

Chris knocked.

No answer.

We banged and shouted but to no avail. I held my ear to the door to listen for any signs of movement. There were none.

Chris grabbed my hand and we walked down the stairs and across the street to the apartment complex office. I explained the situation to a leasing agent who then immediately ran for her manager. I want to be effusive in my praise of the apartment manager that day.

She said that she couldn't allow me in the apartment but that she would go check on him. I didn't realize it then, resigning myself to her "corporate compliance," but she did me the biggest favor by refusing to let me enter that apartment. Bless her heart. I don't know exactly what she saw when she entered that apartment, but I've heard enough to know that it wasn't pretty (and neither was the smell). But she was kind and thoughtful and composed and professional. She didn't even have to say anything as she returned to the office. Sitting on the edge of my seat, I met her gaze. Her eyes said it all. "I'm so sorry for your loss."

People say that death is the great equalizer. They are wrong. Death is THE GREAT DERAILER. No matter how many self-help books you've read, how great your career and your marriage and your family and your self-image and your finances and your health and all the things that are internal and external measures of success and happiness, death can undo it all in just an instant.

I knew Dad was dying. Had been dying of cirrhosis for years. I knew that he had already lived three or five years longer than the doctors predicted. I had even prayed for his death, for the relief from the interminable waiting, and the front row seat to the demise that alcohol was wreaking on his aging body.

It didn't matter that I was mentally prepared for the fact of his dying. You just can't prepare for death. Of course you can prepare for the financial matters and the legal matters and the estate and the burial. But nothing really prepares you for what you feel when you are in it.

Sitting in the leasing office of Dad's apartment complex, I had to get some air. I ran outside and I started crying. I didn't even know why exactly I was crying, but I was crying anyway. My fiancé held me and comforted me. He called his sister to let her know what happened and that we wouldn't be picking up his son as soon as planned. Because we had to stay.

We had to stay while an ambulance was called and EMTs officially pronounced him as deceased.

We had to stay while the police arrived and conducted an investigation to ensure there was no foul play. It was during this time that I learned that there was a significant amount of blood, that he had probably been dead for a week, and that his apartment had been declared a biohazard. Legally, I could enter, but everyone STRONGLY cautioned against it. I heeded their advice.

I started to see neighbors that I had known and who knew my father. One guy wailed and cried. These people who knew my father at the end, they loved him. I'm thankful that at the end there were people who loved him as he was and who were devastated by his death. I'm thankful that he had such good friends.

I started to get questions from the neighbors I had texted the previous evening. I had to break the news to them.

I had a conversation with the apartment manager about logistics. It would take a week or so to make the apartment enterable and then they would give me as much time as I needed to remove my father's belongings. The bed, however, was in itself a hazard and would have to be removed and destroyed.

Grief, sadness, logistics, plans, relief, sadness, numbness. A sense of being outside the realm of space and time and yet still very cognizant of just how much time had passed.

I think I called Mom. I guess I had to have called Mom. I think I had reached out to her the night before to see if she had heard from Dad. She told me that he had wished her a "Happy Birthday" on October 29 and that was the last she had heard from him.

My dad's story is tragic. So much wasted potential. Such intelligence squandered. Such a desire to do right but a rigidity of personality that never allowed him to learn from his mistakes or to recover from setbacks.

Yet, his final words on this earth were to wish my mom, his ex-wife and the love of his life, a happy birthday.

Lesson #20: Choose GRACE: Giving Radical Acceptance and Compassion Enthusiastically.

There are a lot of lessons to be learned or topics to discuss, but there is just one that I think is crucial to share with you. Choose GRACE.

My dad was a difficult man. He was an alcoholic and physically abusive. He was disillusioned and inauthentic. He was a liar and a deceiver. But I LOVED HIM.

He was also funny and smart. He loved Motown Music and where other people like to "dance," Dad liked to "boogie." He loved fish and aquariums and his saltwater tank was one of his greatest sources of pride until he became too sick to maintain it.

He loved the outdoors and water volleyball and burgers from the grill.

I loved listening to his stories. He was THE ULTIMATE STORYTELLER and wordmaster. Maybe, by this point, you will start to see that so many of my own gifts are ones I received from him.

For all of his flaws, and there were many, he ALWAYS told me that "I could do and be anything I wanted in life." While so many women I know had fathers who treated them as if their only importance was to be pretty or that women were inferior to men, my father always believed that I could do anything the boys my age could do. He always complimented my intelligence. Even in my lowest moments, I had an innate belief in myself and my own intelligence because of the repetitions that my father instilled in me.

What does any of this have to do with Lesson #20?

On that day at his apartment complex, dealing with all the complexities of his "shuffle off this mortal coil," and all of the MANY emotions that I felt that day, there is one that was missing: regret.

As I mentioned before, Dad had been my roommate for a short period in the years prior to his passing. He even became my friend. In that last decade before he died, I forgave him, over and over and over again. I forgave him in my heart and I forgave him in my words. I forgave him in my actions.

I had the chance to talk out some (not all) of my childhood trauma. I heard his side of the story. He was able to listen to mine and even apologized for some of his actions. I truly believe that he was a man who tried his best. I know that he was a man who, as bad as it was, was able to do better by me than his own father had done by him.

In the months after he died, I would struggle with grief. I would be encumbered by the logistics of moving his possessions. I would even reach out to a therapist for help. I would feel as if dementors were in every room, stealing the color and happiness from every experience. I would want to call him and grab one last margarita with him. I would wish that he had written the book he always wanted to write so that I could have his words to hold on to. I would also find relief that I no longer had to worry about his health and well-being.

But most of all, I would feel peace. True peace. A knowledge that I had done everything in my power emotionally, mentally, and physically for my father, for someone I had loved so deeply in spite of how challenging he made it. I had no regrets. Because I had no regrets, I was left with untainted memories of the good times that we had together. To this day there is still sadness and grief and longing, but most importantly, peace.

This is a story of my troubled relationship with my father, but I think there's a message that's even bigger than that. The true message that I want to share with you.

I have always believed that Love Wins. I believe it more now than I ever have.

My father is the only person that I have ever truly hated. He caused me a lot of hurt in my life and I have spent a lot of time in therapy dealing with the repercussions of our interactions.

Yet, with him, I found GRACE. I gave him radical acceptance. I treated him with compassion. I did it of my own volition and I did it enthusiastically.

My father is worthy of love – as we all are. I am blessed to have been able to be a conduit of this radical love. If I could come to love him, give him grace, treat him with compassion, then I can offer that to anyone.

Don't take this the wrong way. Go back to previous stories in this book. I could not change him and part of loving him meant having VERY strong boundaries in place in our relationship.

But LOVE ALWAYS WINS. Love is more powerful than any other force. We have the ability to choose to tap into it or not.

I did it for him and I did it for me. Choosing GRACE and choosing love has played a major part in my own empowerment. Forgiveness is a choice and choosing it has helped me to become a stronger, better person. It has helped me to know peace.

Mahatma Gandhi says, "Be the change you wish to see in the world." I believe this world needs peace and love. It needs radical acceptance and compassion. It begins with me. I hope you choose it too.

So, my dear fabulous divine traveler, how can you choose GRACE?

~21~

Man, She Was Dripping Sweat

2000, 2017

I was sitting in our school cafeteria with my JV soccer teammates, our parents, our dates, and the Varsity soccer team and their families and their dates. We were wearing dresses instead of uniforms, strappy sandals instead of cleats, makeup instead of sunscreen, and sparkly hair clips instead of ponytails. It was the Spring awards banquet and we were dressed up and ready to celebrate the season's achievements.

Coach Springer announced the MVP, as well as a few other awards. Then, this men's-football-coach-turned-women's-soccer-coach started to announce the next award.

"Our next award, the Fighting Heart Award, goes to a hard-working young lady. She hustles and always gives 110%. In fact, when practice is over, all the other girls are just glistening, but KIM STORY – MAN SHE IS DRIPPING SWEAT!"

There was silence in the cafeteria as every single player, her family, and her date all looked around for the source of all this sweat.

It was me.

My face turned as pink as the dress I was wearing. How could my toned legs somehow have transformed into jelly? Why couldn't I have won the MVP, Best Offense, or Best Defense? No, I had to win the award for the most sweat!

I couldn't sit in my chair any longer. I had to walk up to the stage while the giggles followed in my wake. My coach was so proud of me and so proud of his introduction, his face beaming, oblivious to my desire to disappear. (Where was Bilbo's ring when I truly needed it?!)

I accepted my award with as much grace as I could muster and sank back into my chair.

As embarrassed as I was at the moment, it was true. I was proud of my Fighting Heart Award and proud of my sweat. I was proud that when the coach told us to run laps – but he wasn't looking – and EVERY SINGLE ONE of my teammates would cut corners, I never did. I ran every step around every 90 degree turn. I wasn't the fastest and I wouldn't come in first, but I never cut corners.

Dad had told me, "always end strong" and "leave it all out on the field." When my teammates would start walking if they heard the whistle, I would jog back to the bench. I was never the most talented. I certainly wasn't born with the most skill. But I always gave 110%. I never held anything back. I always finished strong. Today, I am still proud of that Fighting Heart Award.

Lesson #21: Success is not perfection, success is sweat.

There is a saying, "Don't Ever Let Them See You Sweat." It has a great meaning and certainly there is a lesson to be learned.

But I believe that SUCCESS IS SWEAT. Success is hard work and effort. Success is discipline. Success means getting a little dirty. Success means being tough and unafraid of a little competition.

When I was in high school, I came across Henry David Thoreau's book, *Walden* (Thoreau 2008). He tells us, "I went to the woods because I wished to live deliberately, to front only the essential facts of life, and see if I could not learn what it had to teach, and not, when I came to die, discover that I had not lived."

WOW! What powerful words about life! What is life? How can we avoid life that is not actually living?

Then he says, "I wanted to live deep and suck out all the marrow of life." At that time I didn't really know what marrow was. It was explained to me that it is the meat that is inside the bones. It is full of fat and nutrients and goodness and it can, in fact, be sucked out of a T-bone steak you are eating.

Later I would discover bone marrow transplants and how that can provide life-saving healing and energy to the recipient.

I'm not a doctor, so please don't take me too literally in all this. I just want you to take a moment and sit with this visual. I want you to sit with the question, "What does it mean to *suck out* ALL the marrow of life?"

This visual is intimate, purposeful, and messy.

Just like passion.

Just like sweat.

A few years ago, I was serving as a Toastmasters Area Director, supporting five clubs in the Coppell and Lewisville areas of DFW. Today was our spring speech contest and I had been given the afternoon slot.

2:00 p.m. In April. In Texas.

It was a sunny day and I was wearing a skirt suit. I couldn't start bringing in the materials for my contest until the two earlier contests had completed.

I loaded items from my SUV onto the dolly. I rolled it along the hot concrete. It was then I remembered that black may be slimming, it may be professional, but it is also FUCKING HOT!

I immediately felt the beads begin to form in all the places. My thighs became slick. Droplets slithered down my spine to settle into the waistband of my underwear. My face began to "glisten" (remember that Kim Story doesn't *actually* "glisten").

Don't ever let them see you sweat.

SURE! As if!

I was sweating profusely, in my suit, red-faced, as I got everything situated for the contest. Did it matter that I was sweating? Not one bit. It was a huge success and we had a lot of fun!

My friends and I still laugh about that day.

Passion is sweaty. Passion is not perfection.

For you to be the person you are meant to be, to pursue your passions, to suck out all the marrow of life, don't be afraid to sweat!

So, my dear fabulous divine traveler, which of your passions are going to require some sweat?

~22~

But Where Do You Go to Cry?

2020

I became a stepmom, to a fifth-grade boy, who was doing online school, in the middle of the pandemic.

Let me repeat.

During the summer of 2020, I moved in with Chris and his ten-year-old son, who was still attending school virtually.

To say it was a difficult year is…an understatement.

While I had dated other men who had children, I did not have any biological children of my own. This was me, becoming a mother for the first time.

Sidenote, it was during this time that all the crying and acting out, (mine, surprisingly, not my stepson's) did help me find inspiration. If I ever create a heavy metal band, I will absolutely be calling it Tears and Tantrums.

I was still working nights and weekends, in-person, in the tutoring industry, but because of the move, my commute had doubled, from 25 minutes to 50 minutes, each way.

I must really love this man.

Two weeks into the school year, I left for work in tears. I cried the whole 50 minutes there. Clocked in. Checked in with my reports, spent an hour working, and then told my boss I needed a personal day. I went home, my face still blotchy from all of the earlier crying.

It was then that I started to panic. I messaged my girlfriends, "Where do you go to cry?"

Only six weeks before, I had been living alone in my two-story townhome. Just me and my cat. When I was upset, I had options. I could cry in the living room. I could cry in the bedroom. I could cry in the bathroom. I could even cry in the living room — and no one would be the wiser.

But now I was living with Chris and with a ten-year-old boy. Where was I supposed to go to cry?

I was crying in my car while my married-with-kids girlfriends offered the obvious suggestions: car, bathtub, and closet. I tried out all three.

I went for a walk and cried some more.

As I was walking back along the sidewalk and closing in on our driveway, I thought to myself, "I love Chris. But I could leave, right now. I could set out, on foot, and leave all of my earthly possessions behind. I will follow whichever deity will take me, as long as I don't have to go back to that house."

> *Is this how Jesus got his followers? I really want to know.*
> *Did each of them have a preteen at home?*
> *"So, you're saying I get to leave home for three-to-five years, in the name of God, because it's HIS will? Where do I sign up?!"*

A few weeks later, I changed jobs so that I could also work from home.

A few weeks after that, Chris and I were engaged.

And only two weeks after our engagement, my father died.

I have written other chapters on grief and the lessons I learned from it. This is about the difficult times that we went through, with Chris and I and his son learning how to live together. The times when I second-guessed my every action and inaction during those first few months. The times when I created an emotional Fight Club, beating myself up in my mind on a consistent basis.

(The only rule about Emotional Fight Club is that we NEVER talk about Emotional Fight Club – Let the self-flagellation BEGIN!)

I started therapy. We got married. I lost my job. I got rehired at my former job, commuting 45 minutes away. My stepson adopted a kitten, making us a four-cat household. I changed jobs again. My husband was hospitalized for a week while he had multiple procedures resulting in his gallbladder being removed.

At one point, my stepson and I were in the living room talking. I don't know what made him bring it up, but he said to me, "You really need to be nicer to Dad. He's pretty good to you."

It would have been kinder if he had stabbed me in the heart with actual daggers. Hearing those words, after all the many sacrifices I had made for him and for his dad and the tears I had cried because of the innumerable unmet expectations I had experienced, was DEVASTATING. My heart was pained… because I took it to heart.

However, in true Toastmasters fashion I replied, "Thank you for the feedback."

What does empowerment look like when you feel powerless? How can you be empowered when your heart hurts? When the burning question that you ask is *"Where do I go to cry?"*

I don't have all the answers, but I will say that time and time and time again, during those months that led into these first couple of years together, there was one piece of advice that I heard over and over and over again.

Lesson #22: Don't be so hard on yourself.

I think that we as women are so good at being so hard on ourselves. And in no years has this been more true than in 2020–2021.

We put so much work into our relationships, into our kids, into our looks, into our jobs, and yet, it still doesn't really give us any more control.

We can't control our kids, our jobs, our spouses, our friends, our families, our governments, or our society any more than we can control illness or ex-wives.

But we try. And we fail. So we try harder. And then we are even more devastated when it doesn't work.

I know. I did it. I cried over it.

(If this were *Clue,* it would be "Ms. Story, with the Kleenex, in the Closet.")

I don't know who needs to hear this today but don't be so hard on yourself. In fact, let's flip it around. Be kind to yourself.

This is even deeper than self-care (which is important) or affirmations (which are helpful). How can you love yourself? How can you be kinder to yourself? How can you treat yourself as if you are important? How can you come to believe that you do matter and that all of the little things, the caring, thoughtful, unappreciated things that you do for the people around you — those things matter too?

How can we find our love from within instead of beating ourselves up when we don't earn it from others?

I am here to tell you that you are a part of the divine. You came from spirit and you are spirit and to spirit you will return. You are eternal.

You are not the center of this world, but you are a powerful co-creator in it.

You are important. You are peace and energy. You are kindness. You are thoughtfulness. You are beauty. You are love.

Your actions matter, but not more so than the still, quiet voice that connects your heart and mind and soul.

There is no pressure. Only peace.

No stress. Only peace.

No worry. Only peace.

No disappointment. Only peace.

You are peace. Don't be so hard on yourself. Be at peace. Be kind to yourself.

So, my dear fabulous divine traveler, can you stop being so hard on yourself?

~23~

Dolphins Are My Spirit Animal

1998

It was just me and the therapist. She invited me further into the room. It was our first one-on-one session.

We had met as a family previously. During THAT session I had been the one to tell my dad that my mom had been talking about divorcing him. He was SHOCKED. I didn't know it was a secret. She had been telling me she was going to leave him since I was in fifth grade. In fact, I had begged her to leave him. Now, as a high school student, I had assumed it was common knowledge that she wanted to leave. I was wrong. Once again, I had made things worse instead of better. I was just being honest. But honesty got me in trouble and hurt the people around me.

Now it was just me and the therapist. She asked me to sit on a sofa in her office. I remember there being a pink, rose pattern on the beige sofa, but I could be making it up. The room wasn't too bright or too dark. Too warm or too cold. I was comfortable.

She told me we were going to do an exercise. She brought out a thick stack of cards. It was probably four times the size of a deck of playing cards, so I'm going to assume there were at least 150 cards to choose from. She explained that they each had a picture of an animal on them and that I was to choose which one resonated with me the most. That it would help her to understand more about me.

Well, she found out I was meticulous and followed directions and worried about being "right." I spent almost the entirety of our session going through each card, analyzing it, and keeping it or setting it aside. I narrowed down the choices. It was difficult with so many to choose from. I feel like there was even a unicorn card. The cards were also very pretty and I liked looking at the images.

Eventually, after an eternity, I chose a dolphin. I loved sea creatures and dolphins are intelligent and majestic.

That's the only thing I remember about that session. I spent an entire therapy session to choose a dolphin. There wasn't any additional insight that I gained from that experience and if the therapist gained any, she didn't share it with me.

I told my mom about it after. I don't know exactly how much this therapist was charging, but I know it was a lot because we had received the referral from another attorney my dad knew. I told my mom it was a waste of time and I didn't want to go back.

We didn't.

However, we still had so many issues at home, and I had so many issues in my head. I decided to visit some Al-Anon meetings – support groups for children of alcoholics. I found it to be a safe place to meet with other people experiencing similar challenges to my own. It didn't fix everything, but it did remind me that it was okay to get help and to look for ways to improve my situation, from the inside out.

2002

It was my sophomore year in college. I was away from home and my sister had been using crystal meth for over a year. Her drug use began to take its toll. I was getting phone calls from her and phone calls from my mom, both sobbing and upset but without resolution. I didn't hear much from my dad. All I knew is that he and my sister were getting into physical altercations and my mom was caught in the middle.

I would go to the church chapel and cry. Just me and Jesus. I was looking for His comfort. I asked God why this was happening. I prayed that he would take my sister's pain and give it to me instead. That's not really how it works, but I do think my prayers for pain were successful.

I found a lot of support in my church group at St. Mary's Catholic Church in College Station, but so few people understood what I was going through. They hugged me and consoled me and cried with me, but they weren't qualified to help me.

Thankfully, as a college student, I was able to get therapy sessions for free on campus. I started meeting with a young male counselor. I deliberately chose a male because I wanted to work through my daddy issues. It was so hard for me to trust a male. It was so hard for me to feel safe. Our sessions were videotaped and my counselor was truly amazing. He was patient and kind and I know we worked through a lot that year. It was a much better experience than I had had previously and it restored my faith in therapy.

I felt like it wasn't fair, though. I had so many issues that weren't my fault, that were caused by others, and now I had to spend so much time dealing with them. Why couldn't I have been born into a different family? One where I didn't have to spend my college years working so hard just to be "normal"? Just so I could function?

My junior year of college I chose co-ed group therapy instead of individual therapy. This was also a good experience. I met a couple of people who became friends outside of therapy. I learned about some of the other challenges that my peers were facing: abortion and homosexuality. (You probably won't assume based on the previous sentence that it was a male who was coming to terms with the effects of his girlfriend's choice to have an abortion and it was a female who was dealing with the challenges of being a lesbian in Texas.)

These were challenges that I didn't relate to. It wasn't that my problems were bigger or smaller than others, they were just different. I hadn't experienced many of the challenges that others in the group were facing and for that I could be grateful. Isn't that the way of it, though? Each of us has challenges that we face in this human experience? It's not about an emotional pissing contest – my problems are worse than your problems – but rather that we are all human. Sometimes the negative emotions we feel and challenges we face, well, we can choose to let them unify us in our humanity or divide us in our enmity.

It was many years before I started going to therapy again. I was just so tired and felt it was so unfair. I was also poor, without health insurance, and felt I couldn't afford it.

Why did I have so many issues? Why had I started life so far behind the starting line of so many of my peers? Why did I have to spend the time and money for therapy when so many other people didn't? It wasn't fair.

But what is so great, is that it was there available, waiting, when I needed it.

Summer 2017

In 2017, when I moved out of the apartment my dad and I were sharing and he told me it would be my fault that he would be homeless, I went to Al-Anon meetings again. The first one I went to, I just cried the whole time I was there. These were my

134

people and they understood the challenges I was facing. I wasn't alone. I had community and a safe place to cry.

December 2020

When we were dealing with the pandemic and job uncertainty, when I had moved in with Chris and his son, when we had gotten engaged but found out only a week and a half later that my dad had passed, I started going to therapy again. Chris, this amazing, beautiful, wise, caring man, said to me, "I love you but I'm not qualified to help you."

February 2021

"Well, I'm just so angry that my stepson doesn't unload the dishwasher."

"Kim, what are you afraid of?"

"What do you mean, what am I afraid of? I told you that I'm angry."

"Kim, in my experience as a therapist, if someone is feeling this emotional, this angry, it's usually rooted in fear. So, Kim, what are you afraid of? What will happen if your stepson doesn't unload the dishwasher?"

"He'll end up a drug addict like my sister."

WAIT. WHAT? WHOAH!

This was just one of MANY breakthroughs that my therapist and I had. Realizing that I had an irrational fear that if my stepson didn't do his chores then he wouldn't have structure and discipline and therefore, he would end up like my sister. My deepest fear is having to live through that experience again. To love someone so much and watch them destroy themselves. I was terrified of having it live out again in front of me, in the form of my stepson.

I would never have been able to figure this out on my own, but figuring it out has made life for me, my husband, my stepson, and our household so much better.

Lesson #23: It's okay to ask for help. It's also necessary to choose from whom you get the help.

This chapter wasn't a part of my original vision for this book. I didn't think it was necessary. But I realized that some of the other stories left gaps, and that there was a desire to know more about the part that therapy has had in my life.

Right now there is a lot of discussion about mental health. In fact, as I write this, Mental Health Awareness Day was only earlier this week. I love this. I love that we are removing the stigma that if you go to therapy, something is wrong with you. We don't need to ask, "What's wrong with you that you need therapy?"

Now that I have had more experiences, I would be asking the question, "What's so right with you that you are willing to do this work to improve yourself?" or "How much do you love the people around you that you are willing to get the help you need?"

I was raised with the value of independence. I loved hearing people tell me how strong I was. Being strong was a large part of my identity. Being independent and doing things on my own was strength, right? Not ever needing help was being strong and that's empowerment, yeah?

Not exactly.

Learning the skill of asking for help has not been easy for me, but it's been necessary.

I don't like it when other people assume that I'm a mind-reader and that I know what they want without their telling me. So why would I do it to others?

It is okay to ask for help. In fact, it is crucial. We are not alone and we were not designed to be alone. We have sayings such as, "It takes a village to raise a child." The more I learn the more I realize that the biggest goals and most amazing feats are accomplished with a team. I have heard, "If your goal only needs you to accomplish it, maybe you need a bigger goal."

When it comes to mental health and living a healthy life, you've got to put the oxygen mask on yourself first. You cannot help others if you don't take care of yourself. It is okay to ask for help. But it's also important to choose who you are asking. It is important to respect when someone says, "I love you but I'm not qualified to help you." My depression and anxiety were too big for my husband. He wasn't qualified. I needed a professional. When I asked for help from a professional, the results were PHENOMENAL.

In 2021, within only a few sessions my therapist and I made major progress. She helped me recognize my irrational fears that were negatively impacting my life and the lives of those I loved. She helped me to have compassion for the limits of others and to retract the expectations I had of them – expectations that they would never be able to fulfill.

In 2022, my husband and I started going to couple's therapy to work through the challenges of our blended family. Once again, with professional and objective help, we were able to discover new ways of listening, communicating, compromising, and following through. Our marriage is stronger because we chose to ask for help and because we made our relationship a priority.

So, my dear fabulous divine traveler, whom do you need to ask for help?

~24~

Nights, Weekends, and Blackout Dates

2016–present

"I'm sorry I can't go; I have to work."

For yet another year, I wasn't going to be able to go to my family's annual reunion in the Smoky Mountains of Tennessee.

My mother's family is from Cleveland, Tennessee, and ever since I was a kid, my family would get together on Lake Ocoee and go boating, canoeing, hiking, and white-water rafting. I love the mountains and the lake. When I travel to a vantage point on Chilhowee Mountain and look out at the vista before me, I know God. My heart is home.

My mom is one of six children, so seeing my grandparents, aunts, uncles and dozens of cousins was always a highlight for me. Growing up so far away in Dallas, I didn't always feel connected to my extended family. I was jealous of my cousins who grew up close enough to be friends and be active in each other's lives. Every summer when I traveled to Lake Ocoee as a kid, I would be reminded that I had a family, and I was part of something bigger.

There was so much love and laughter and TONS of story-telling (I'm sure you're shocked by that revelation).

But I couldn't go, again.

For so many years I couldn't go because I was poor. Now I had the money but didn't have the time. Being in the SAT and ACT industry meant that nights, weekends, and especially summer, were our busiest times. When kids were out of school, I had to work.

I loved the company I worked for, but from 2015–2020, I worked every Sunday and at least two evenings. I had seven total days of vacation/sick time and paid time off the week of Christmas and the week of the Fourth of July. From the beginning of June until the beginning of September was blackout dates for travel (with the exclusion of the Fourth of July time off).

I loved what I did. I was able to impact hundreds, probably even thousands of students and their families during the time I worked in the test prep industry. I LOVED helping kids achieve their goals and reveled in their excitement when they got accepted to the college of their choice or received a scholarship. I loved my coworkers, who were all dedicated to the cause of helping others and who also embraced education and teaching.

And yet, it meant I couldn't go to Tennessee to be with my family. As much as I loved my job and loved what I did. As good as I was at it. As respected as I felt and as much as I enjoyed the camaraderie, I knew it would have to change.

I was jealous of Chris, who worked from home AND had something like 25 days of vacation plus sick time.

I had been reading *The Four-Hour Work Week* by Tim Ferriss over and over and over again for a few years and yet, I still didn't have that lifestyle.

I have changed jobs a couple of times since then, always focused on the intention of working from home and having time freedom - as detailed in Ferriss' "Liberation" chapter about achieving lifestyle design.

I can honestly say that I now work fewer hours while making more money than I ever have in my life (and more money than a lot of my friends who work a lot harder than I do). I have had enough success that I have started to be asked how I've done it and have even started to do presentations on *Time Empowerment*. Everywhere I go, women are looking for more help with time management and how to reclaim their time. Well, the time is now!

For specific time freedom strategies, go to www.fuckuptofabulous.com/ time and download the free pdf <u>Killing The Sacred Cow: The To-Do List</u>.

Lesson #24: You CAN build your work around your life and not live your life around your work.

The year 2020 was difficult, as you may know. There was a lot of fear and a lot of shifting that took place. At work I heard "Pivot." In Toastmasters I heard "Pivot." In my head at night I heard Ross from *Friends* shouting "Pivot. Pi-vot. Pivot!" You may feel that 2020 was a year that has left lingering negative consequences for your life, but I am here to offer the flip side of the coin.

It has NEVER been easier for the average person to live a life of Time Empowerment than it is today. Now, in this time period, an amazing thing has happened.

More and more we are being freed of the idea that you must trade your time for dollars. As long as you are an hourly employee, you will never be truly free. As long as you physically have to journey to a job where you clock in and clock out, you will never be truly empowered to live life on your terms. (Don't get me wrong, those jobs may be a stepping stone to get you what you want. They were for me.)

However, the opportunities abound in this day and age to have Time Empowerment. You don't have to start your own business and take all of the chances and work your ass off in a network marketing business for what turns out to be minimum wage – or less – to have the opportunity to take control of your time anymore.

Working from home and freeing yourself from an office is the first step to time empowerment – and it is possible!

Using technology to create results and eliminate arbitrary work – IS POSSIBLE!
Outsourcing the tasks you dislike and doing more of what you do – IS POSSIBLE!
Living a life where you say, "Yes, I can do that. I have the time" – IS POSSIBLE!

You don't have to save all of your life for the end, save it for "retirement." You can begin to live life to the fullest NOW!

I am so thankful to have gone from a life of "No, I can't do that" to "Yes, I can." I can play pickleball at the YMCA on Tuesday afternoon. I can go to my family reunion in Tennessee each summer. I can be there for my stepson if he needs a ride. I can have the time to write my book. I can have the time to volunteer with the women's empowerment group Plaid For Women. I can have the time to read *Padre Rico Padre Pobre* and become fluent in Spanish.

But this isn't about me. It's about you. What would it look like for you to have more time? How often do you hear yourself say, "I'm sorry, I want to but I just don't have time"? How many of your goals and dreams have you delayed? If you died tomorrow, what would you regret?

You may be focused on the "How?" But HOW did Kim do it? HOW can I do it? I'm purposefully not going into the details of the how because I want to emphasize to you right now that the first step is BELIEF. Do you believe that you can have freedom and control of your time? If not, no amount of steps I give you will get you to your goal and if you do, then the steps that worked for me might not be the ones that get you there the fastest. Time empowerment may look different for you than it does for me (I've already discovered this when talking to my husband about the topic).

As mentioned above, I do have some tips I can provide and additional workshops I offer, but for the purposes of this book, I just want to share with you the belief that it is possible. The knowledge that you can have what you desire.

Time is our most valuable commodity and there has never been a better time in all of history to start living the life of your dreams.

So, my dear fabulous divine traveler, can you start living a life of time empowerment?

~25~

The Great Derailer – Part 2

2023

This past February, only a few months ago, things were going well. We enjoyed the holidays and had a great Christmas as a family. We were excited about the New Year. My stepson had earned all A's in online school and seemed to be thriving in that environment. My husband and I were happy, our jobs were secure, we were making headway financially and had even planned our next vacation together to stay in an all-inclusive resort in Los Cabos, the same city where we went on our honeymoon.

Then, my husband's elderly grandmother passed away. We had had a chance to say goodbye to her and knew that she didn't have long for this world. She had stopped recognizing my husband, calling Chris by his father's name instead. She was ready to go.

Why would this have such an impact on me?

I've never been afraid of death. At times in my life, I would have welcomed it. But this aging process. This reminder that this wonderful life that I had built and created, this life that I didn't need to take a vacation from, that it could, and would, all end, was terrifying.

Then, the next week, I found out that one of my mentors from Toastmasters passed away. I had seen her a few months before at the most recent conference. Even though she was in her 70s, Bonne had charisma and energy. She had life and a smile that lit up a room. Her mind was sharp as a tack and she was witty. I had seen her and hugged her, but in the hustle and bustle of the conference, didn't get a chance to really sit down and talk with her.

Now I would never again have that opportunity. It made me so very sad. How quickly Bonne had gotten sick and how she had never recovered. How it came as a shock to all of us.

I knew the impact that Bonne had had on our Toastmasters community. She and I had served in leadership together and on conference committees together. We were members of the same club for a while and I even went to her house once for our club's Christmas party celebration meeting.

I wasn't as close to her as many others. I knew the deep pain that my other friends were feeling, the ones who had been Bonne's confidants. Who had known her for decades instead of just a handful of years like me. I hurt for them. For their loss as much as my own.

I went to two funerals in less than one week.

My husband's ex-wife came to his grandmother's funeral, and I was not in a gracious place. Every time someone said how wonderful and thoughtful it was for her to be there, it made me ill. I was self-conscious about her son sitting up in the front row with my husband and me. I was self-conscious about what my husband's family friends were thinking when we were all standing around talking to each other after the reception. I wanted to grieve without this extra complication. This was MY family, not hers.

I was not in a good place. As you can see, my husband's ex WAS being thoughtful and she IS a part of this family, always will be. My sadness, fear, and grief made me petty.

Then I went to Bonne's funeral. The legacy that this woman left. The people who traveled to be there. The showing of support from our Toastmasters community (at least 50 of us were there), but also her family and her school community and other civic organizations. She had been so involved in so many different organizations. Her life had been such a positive influence on those around her. She had truly made the world a better place.

At her funeral is where I learned about the tragedy she had endured. Becoming a widow, losing the love of her life and her travel companion, stepping up to fill the role of mom AND dad for her young son.

I never knew. I knew she wasn't married, but I never knew that she became a widow in roughly the same year that I was born.

I never knew because she was so full of happiness and life and love and spirit. She didn't carry the shadow of that loss, or at least I never saw it. She did not have bitterness or anger. I didn't see pain, only joy.

She inspired me. I cry as I write this, thinking about what an amazing woman she was. How I wish I had spent more time with her. How I hope to have even the tiniest impact on the world around me and leave a legacy like she did.

My pain and my grief were consuming me. My fear about dying or, even worse, losing my husband, losing the man I loved and had waited so long to be with, was actually detracting from the very relationship I wanted to protect.

I hadn't been going to therapy for a little over a year now. I had gotten to a good place and didn't need it.

But I needed it now.

So, I reached out to the office of my therapist. I sent an email saying that I needed to book an appointment and what was her availability?

A few hours later I received the response. I was dumbfounded. I went into my husband's office. He was in a meeting and I asked him to come speak with me when it was done.

He came into my office and said, "What's up?" He was thinking I was upset with my stepson, again. He was prepared to talk about some family thing.

But I couldn't even respond. There aren't any words. I just held out my phone and told him to read the email.

Thank you for reaching out. Unfortunately, I have some sad news that your therapist actually passed away. It was of natural causes and they believe it was peaceful. We know this can be difficult and understand if you need to take some time to process before making a decision to move forward with counseling. If you are ready to move forward let me know and we can discuss other options.

I watched his face as he read the email. He tried to repress it, but his eyes met mine, we shrugged our shoulders, and in disbelief, we started to nervously chuckle together, then laugh, then guffaw until our eyes watered and our stomachs hurt.

It sounds awful that we laughed, but the wellspring of pent-up grief inside me was finally released by the power of unmitigated irony.

Lesson #25: Sometimes life is fucking ironic.

You can't make this shit up.

Chris thought it felt like a Seinfeld episode, and I felt like I was in an Alanis Morisette song.

I was reaching out to schedule a therapy session to deal with all my grief surrounding death, only to find out my therapist was, in fact, deceased.

Well, now I needed a therapist to deal with the grief from the death of my therapist. Fuuuuuuuuck!

Did my therapist know what an impact she had on my life? How many break-throughs I had because she had been so good at her profession? How much I appreciated her?

What do we do when we have these, "You can't make this shit up" experiences?

For me, I relied on all the other lessons from this book. I "found the funny"…and boy is it (tragically) funny!

I was "grateful in all circumstances." Even in the midst of death and grief and sadness, there was so much to be grateful for. I was grateful for my in-laws and this wonderful family I had married into. I was grateful for my Toastmasters community and the opportunity to meet so many amazing people who are truly doing good in this world. I was grateful for my husband, who was there to laugh with me through it all.

I also "took responsibility for my life." I took responsibility for my grief and sadness and bitterness and fear and anger. I found a new therapist and worked through these feelings with her, even the feelings regarding the death of my previous therapist.

Facing these endings, facing my own mortality and that of the people I loved, also helped me to go back to remember to "create a vision for my dream life." I know what I want and I "trust my intuition" to help me get it.

I want to love my husband, my stepson, my extended family, my friends, and my community and I want to love them well.

I want to make a difference in the world.

I want to use my experiences to inspire others.
I want to leave a legacy.
I want to finish my book.
More than anything, I want to help others to live

AN EMPOWERED LIFE!

I hope, dear divine traveler, that through this book, I have done just that.

~ Bonus Chapter ~
Our Love Story – His Version

About me

So at this point I'm assuming you have a pretty good idea of Kim and possibly even Kim and me, so I'll start by telling you a little about me. I'm the middle child of an electrical engineer and an art teacher, and that's probably the best description of me I could imagine. I work in IT because I can speak to computers, but I'm one of the rare types that can speak to computers and people. I'm pretty knowledgeable in most subjects, in a way that makes me a great asset at trivia night. Well, except for sports, I don't know sports trivia, or sports in general. I will lose every game of Trivial Pursuit because of that damn orange piece. I'm the indoor type, but I don't really have a choice. I'm literally allergic to grass, the whole outdoors is trying to kill me all the time, and on more than one occasion, they've come closer than I care to think about. I'm an indoors person, sunlight is for plants, AC is better than the wind, and WiFi is a human right. I got bullied in Jr. High, and since I couldn't fight very well, I learned to make people laugh. People don't like seeing the funny guy get beaten up; it was a surprisingly good defense mechanism for middle school. I love to make people laugh: I love to make

151

people laugh at themselves, laugh when they're not expecting to, and I love to inject a laugh whenever possible. I also have a severe case of ADHD, which means I'm distracted quite easily and I'm incredibly forgetful. It can be great though. Because I'm bad at memorization, it's made me good at improvisation, since I can't remember what I prepared exactly anyway.

I'm very lucky to have come from a very functional loving family. It's the kind of family that looks like the perfect 80s sitcom family, but it was made up of a bunch of broken pieces. My older brother is actually my half-brother, from my mom's first marriage. Her first husband walked out on her before he was a toddler. My dad married her and raised my brother as his own. You'd never have any sense that there was no blood linking them. I came along later and then my sister. When I was 15, we took in my cousin and she lived with us until she was old enough to move out on her own. The thing is, growing up you'd never know we came from so many parts; we seemed so cohesively whole. It was crazy how well we all meshed together.

If you haven't noticed Kim and I are opposite in just about every way possible. She's sporty and outdoorsy, always prepared, organized, loves being out in the sun, and comes from a trainwreck of a single household. I'm a super-technical, artsy, spontaneous, loud, indoor vampire, with no attention span from a successful blended family. Luckily, we're both really funny and love board games.

Kim and I

I've known Kim since she was probably in junior high and I was in high school. We went to the same church camp together. I'm pretty sure I was a lifeguard when she was a teenage camper. She was 4 years younger than me, and I had no interest in being around her because of her age. One of my more specific memories was when a couple of my friends were throwing a party with a bunch of our former camp friends and providing a keg since we just turned 21. One of my friends wanted to invite Kim, who would not yet have turned 18. I was incredibly vocal about not inviting a minor to this party. "Under no circumstances should Kim Story be invited to this party." I lost the argument, or maybe

I won the argument, but either way Kim found her way to the party anyway. Because, of course she did.

Honestly, I never thought much of her when we were growing up in the same friend group – although separated by about four or five years. We stayed in touch over the years, not directly, but we knew enough of the same people that we would occasionally bump into each other. When I ran a computer repair department at Fry's Electronics – if you're not familiar with it, imagine a store the size of a Walmart filled with everything you'd find at a Best Buy, RadioShack, and GameStop – her dad worked in the AV section as coordinator. As a retail director, I still had to walk the aisles and tell him what he needed to do differently. Just one of the many ways our paths had crossed. I met her dad without even knowing it.

I got married and Kim became a friend of my wife. We threw a house party game night and invited a bunch of friends. Kim was invited. Kim also decided to bring her sister with her. I didn't know her but didn't see a problem with her showing up. After all, Kim was fun, her sister was probably cool, too. Well, I went to check on my bar a little later and found out Kim's sister had gotten into some of the liquor that wasn't supposed to be shared at the party, broken glasses and a bottle behind my bar, caused some sort of scene, and was now throwing up in my kid's bathroom sink. I was pissed, and my near infinite patience was running on empty. Someone I hadn't invited to my party had broken some of my stuff, finished off some liquor that was hidden away and then broke the bottle for it, and pissed off some of the other guests. This was a party in my thirties, I was long past those types of shenanigans, especially from a guest we didn't even invite. So, after I finished sweeping up the mess, I went to confront Kim who was cleaning up after her sister in the bathroom. While I don't remember exactly what I said (I'm sure she does), the tone was pretty mean, and she didn't take it well. I think the next time I saw her, she was engaged. I met her fiancé, who seemed nice enough at the time.

Some years later, I was going through a divorce and my wife left me in the big house we bought together. One of my friends asked to have their anniversary party at my house, since it's large and has a pool. Kim and her fiancé were invited as well as a handful of other friends. Kim and I hit it off really well that night. She was surprised how well I was doing through my divorce. We struck up conversation and started to keep in touch past that night. I knew her engagement wasn't going well, since her wedding had already been delayed twice. Turns out she wanted to know how I was dealing with my divorce because she was working on a way to leave her fiancé. Shortly after we found ourselves both having just got out of or working our way out of long-term relationships. I knew enough about bad relationships to know it was a terrible idea to get together. I was still trying to work on myself after my divorce, and she was trying to find her new stability. I had 50% custody of my son and really wasn't looking at trying to get into a serious relationship, especially when we were both on the rebound. The last thing I wanted was to go through another breakup and, this time, with someone in my friend circle. We had hardly any divorcees in our friend group, and I was just about the first. If the relationship with Kim didn't work, it would be considered wholly my fault. To put it into TV terms, I didn't want to become the "Ross" of our Friends group.

So, through the next couple years we dated each other and we both also dated other people but nobody really that seriously. I was still adamant that we were probably not meant to be together and that I wasn't ready to settle down again. I also didn't want to be in a serious relationship with someone who just got out of a serious relationship; I didn't think we'd be stable together. Kim and I would be off-and-on but would often still find ourselves spending a lot of time together. During this time, I had decided to try new things and say yes to things I wouldn't have done before, in order to grow more, and keep busy. It's how I ended up being the only white guy in an Asian board game group. One night at a party, Kim and I and a few friends were hanging out. It was the end of the party time, that time where most everyone has left or gone to sleep, and the few diehards are there refusing to let the night end. One of our friends, Sara, who I had known since middle school and was recently divorced, said she was wanting to do a trip to Mexico. She had a place to stay with a friend in Mexico City who had plenty of room for all of us, and we would be welcome there. This to me sounded pretty cool and a lot of fun, but in my experience most plans made after 2:00 a.m. at a party rarely come to pass, so I agreed to it, but thought it would go nowhere. Well, I was wrong. It turns out this trip was happening and our friend Sara had planned it all out. From the group of friends that night, it ended up only being three of us going: Kim, myself, and Sara all going to Mexico City to stay with a friend of Sara's I had never met. The trip was amazing! We made new friends, we all got along together, and we got to see so many new and fun experiences – but something funny happened on that trip. Sometimes when you take something and take it out of the environment you're used to, you can see something in a different perspective. Suddenly, being in a whole different location, I could see things I never saw before. I really got to see how Kim and I worked together, and how alike we were, how compatible we were in our adventures, and how much comfort we found in each other. Being in a new place, with new surroundings, and new places to discover, it made me realize that I didn't want to do these things with anyone else. It took me taking this vacation to see something I couldn't see before. I knew before that trip was over that we would get married. (Not that I told Kim).

However, before we got married, we had a bunch of challenges we apparently needed to get through first: a pandemic, moving in together, buying a house, the death of her father, and changing of jobs. Let's just say we got through a lot of stressors in a really short time at the start of our relationship. But there's no one I'd rather go through them with. Kim is my person and I know that "We're so lucky."

And our story, our Haagen Story, it's just beginning.

The Ship

A soul-searching ship was lost at sea,
Could not find the truthfulness lee,
But courage of insight and a paradigm shift,
Forbade that ship from going adrift.
For avast a new rudder that loving vessel has found,
Soul-searching still but for real happiness is now bound.
Cliff Story, 1948–2020

List of Chapters and Lessons

If Anyone Ever Knew You
Lesson #1: Trust your intuition.

I'm Calling the Police
Lesson #2: It's never too late to change.

My Greatest Disappointment
Lesson #3: Choose your friends wisely.

Are You Insane?!
Lesson #4: The formula for success is Be–Do–Have.

First Place Goes To....
Lesson #5: 90% of success is showing up.

I'm So Fascinated
Lesson # 6 Change your words, change your life.

I'm Just Lucky To Be Alive
Lesson #7: Be grateful, in ALL circumstances.

I Love My Life!
Lesson #8: Create a vision for your dream life.

The Path to Toastmasters
Lesson #9: One step at a time.

Riverdance
Lesson #10: Find the funny.

Cat Ransom
Lesson #11: There is life after an ending.

The Nerd Chapter
Lesson #12: To be empowered, be a reader.

Farts Help My Prayer Life
Lesson #13: To be empowered and authentic, own your embarrassing moments.

Destroyer of Corporate Culture
Lesson #14: Take responsibility for your life.

A Final Message

Now that you have read so many of the stories of my life, you will know that I understand pain and anger, fear and sadness.

However, I believed then and I believe even more deeply today, that LOVE WINS.

Love is bigger than pain. Love cures sadness and quells anger. It rights wrongs and melts hearts.

We don't fight anger with anger or fear with more fear.

We conquer it with love, hope, faith, kindness, gratitude, peace, respect, and laughter. This is my focus. This is the message, more than any other that I want to share with the world - LOVE WINS.

Will you focus on the good in the world? Will you use your empowerment to bring peace to the lives of those you meet? Will you choose to be kind and generous, regardless of how you are treated in return? Will you choose to respect the dignity of EVERY person? Will you leave a legacy of hope and laughter?

Dear, fabulous, divine traveler, will you choose LOVE?

References

Byrne, Rhonda. 2006. *The secret.* New York: Atria Books.

Carnegie, Dale 1888-1955. 2009. *How to win friends and influence people.* New York: Simon & Schuster.

Chapman, Gary D. 2010. *The five love languages: the secret to love that lasts.* Chicago: Northfield Publishing.

Cloud, Henry and John Townsend. 1992. *Boundaries: When to say yes, how to say no to take control of your life.* Grand Rapids: Zondervan.

Ferriss, Tim. 2007. *The 4-hour work week: escape 9-5, live anywhere, and join the new rich.* New York: Crown Publishers.

Kiyosaki, Robert T. and Sharon L. Lechter. 1998. *Rich dad poor dad.* New York: Warner Books.

Thoreau, Henry David. 2008. *Walden.* New York: Fall River Press.

Trudeau, Kevin. 2009. "Your Wish Is Your Command." The Global Information Network.

Young, William P. 2007. *The shack.* Newbury Park: Windblown Media.

Made in the USA
Coppell, TX
05 May 2025

49020850R00098